JACK LONDON

A BIOGRAPHY

DANIEL DYER

Scholastic Press / New York

For Prudence and Edward,
my mother and father

All rights reserved.
Published by Scholastic Press, a division of Scholastic Inc.,
Publishers since 1920.

SCHOLASTIC and SCHOLASTIC PRESS and associated logos
are trademarks and/or registered trademarks of Scholastic Inc.

Library of Congress Cataloging-in-Publication Data

Dyer, Daniel (Daniel Osborn), 1944–
Jack London : a biography / by Daniel Dyer. — 1st American ed.
p. cm.
Includes bibliographical references and index.
Summary: Biography of the colorful American writer who had been a
pirate, a seal hunter, a mill worker, a hobo, and a political activist before
becoming a popular author at the age of twenty-nine.
ISBN 0-590-22216-3
1. London, Jack, 1876–1916 — Biography — Juvenile literature. 2. Authors, American — 20th century — Biography — Juvenile literature.

PS3523.O46Z6227   1997
813'.52—dc21   [B] 96-29910

12 11 10 9 8 7 6 5 4 3 2 1   7 8 9/9 0/0 01 02 03

Printed in the U.S.A.   37
First printing, October 1997

Book design by Elizabeth B. Parisi
The display faces are Old Typewriter and Franklin Gothic Heavy.
The text face is Goudy.

CONTENTS

P R E F A C E

June–July 1894: Niagara Falls

It was a living hell, that prison. . . .
— Jack London, *The Road*

The Erie County Penitentiary was not a pleasant place. Erected in 1847 along the banks of the Erie Canal in Buffalo, New York, the great stone prison was divided into four sections. The largest, called "bums' hall," held homeless people and was designed to accommodate 500 men in 230 tiny cells stacked atop one another like animal cages. In the summer of 1894, one of these cells held an eighteen-year-old youth whose name appears in the Record of Prisoners as *John Lundon*. "John Lundon" was a tramp who had been arrested on June 29 in nearby Niagara Falls, New York. His crime was vagrancy.

More than two months earlier, he had left his home in Oakland, California, and traveled across the country by train — without buying a ticket. At times he sneaked into empty boxcars. At other times he hid beneath them, lying flat on his stomach on the under-carriage, riding for dangerous hours close to the rails that roared by his nose. Known to his fellow hoboes as "Sailor Kid" or "Sailor Jack," he had been lucky all along the way. Rarely had the railroad detectives — the *bulls*, as they were called — managed to find him. But in June his luck ran out.

He had spent the night in a field near Niagara Falls, and when he awoke early that Friday morning, he walked into town to beg for food. Unfortunately for him, the first people he encountered were two fellow tramps . . . and the policeman who had just arrested them. The officer insisted that Sailor Kid join the party.

Justice was swift. When Police Justice Charles Piper asked the bailiff for the charge, the response was the same in every case: "Vagrancy, your honor." In every case Piper declared: "Thirty days." Sailor Kid estimated each case took about thirty seconds to complete. When his own turn came, he tried to interrupt — to defend himself. Justice Piper told him to shut up.

The Erie County Penitentiary, near Niagara Falls, New York

As soon as the cases were over, he was handcuffed to another prisoner, then linked by chains to the others and paraded through the streets to the train station. After a fifteen-mile train ride from Niagara Falls to the outskirts of Buffalo, the prisoners were transferred to a streetcar that took them to the Erie County Penitentiary. Inside, Sailor Kid and the others were forced to strip and bathe, for, as he wrote, "the prison swarmed with vermin." Then to the prison barber, where it took only about three minutes for his head to become "as smooth as a billiard ball just sprouting a crop of bristles." Then they were marched in lockstep to their cells. Dinner that night was a couple of chunks of dry bread and some "soup" — a quart of lightly salted warm water with what Sailor Kid called "a lonely drop of grease" floating on the surface.

Early next morning, he and the others were marched outside to the nearby Erie Canal, where they unloaded boats all day. Guards stood by with repeating rifles and machine guns. When Sailor Kid asked one of the guards if he could see a lawyer, the guard laughed.

As his month passed, Sailor Kid learned to trade and barter for things in prison — cigarettes, money, mail. He became hardened to the cruelty and brutality all around him in what he later called "a living hell." He wrote about one deranged man who caught sparrows and ate them alive: "I have seen him crunching bones and spitting out feathers. . . ." He saw a young African American thrown down five flights of stairs for the crime of insisting on fairness. He saw grown men screaming and howling in fits of rage and despair; guards threw buckets of water on them to calm them. When problems arose with other prisoners, Sailor Kid learned to hit first . . . and fast. "My own rule," he wrote, "was to hit a man as soon as he opened his mouth — hit him hard, hit him with anything. A broom-handle, end-on, in the face, had a very sobering effect."

When his sentence was finally up on July 29, 1894, Sailor Kid went into the city of Buffalo, begged money for beer, then hopped a southbound train. Illegally. Prison had not changed his travel plans.

"John Lundon" — or "Sailor Kid" or "Sailor Jack" — was, of course, John Griffith "Jack" London, who by 1904, just ten years after his term in the Erie County Penitentiary, was one of the most popular, highest-paid authors in the world.

It has been occasionally written that the best novel Jack London ever wrote was the story of his own life. It is not hard to explain such an attitude, for Jack London led a remarkable — even astonishing — life. Into a little less than forty-one years, he stuffed enough excitement and accomplishment to satisfy several ordinary people.

Yet he was born into what we today would probably call a "disadvantaged family." His parents did not have much income, and even as a small child he was expected to earn money. He had very little schooling. At that time, eighth grade marked the end of formal education for many people, and Jack London was no exception. At the age of seventeen he sailed to the Sea of Japan on a seal-hunting expedition. At the age of eighteen he was a hobo — illegally boarding trains and riding all over the country. After he returned home to California, he threw himself into an exhausting routine of study and self-improvement. At nineteen he enrolled as a high school freshman. He wanted to be a writer. But everything he wrote — every single thing — was rejected by publishers.

In the summer of 1897 — just as Jack was about to give up his dream — word came that there had been a fabulous gold strike in the Canadian Yukon on the tributaries of a little-known river called the Klondike. With the help of his brother-in-law, he headed north in search of gold.

And he found it. Not in the ground, but in the experiences he had during his year in the Yukon. When he returned home in the summer of 1898, he was brimming with ideas to write about. Once again he tried to succeed as a writer, and once again he had little success. And then . . . slowly at first . . . his writing began to sell.

Within five years, Jack was a successful writer, his work appearing in the nation's finest magazines and newspapers. Within ten years, he was the most popular writer in the world — and one of the highest-paid, too. Before his life ended in 1916, his writing would earn him all the comforts of life — from yachts to a fourteen-hundred-acre ranch in a beautiful California valley. His writing would send him to fascinating places. He would attempt to sail his own boat around the world. He would be an international celebrity. And his books would be studied in the very schools where he had been a student only years earlier.

It is easy to see why some people think that Jack London's life was his best story. But this is not a fair characterization, for he wrote some books that have endured as American classics — *The Sea-Wolf*, *Martin Eden*, and *White Fang*. And his tale *The Call of the Wild* is one of the most popular and respected novels in world literature. His short stories continue to appear in literature anthologies in schools and colleges all over the world — especially "To Build a Fire," "All Gold Canyon," "War," "The White Silence," and "A Piece of Steak."

Some of his lesser known works continue to read well today, too. His futuristic novel, *The Iron Heel*, is a horrifying vision of a world in the control of a rigid central government. *Before Adam* is a novel about prehistoric people. *The Star Rover* is a fascinating tale of a prisoner whose spirit leaves his body during torture sessions and travels through time and space, "remembering" past lives. *John Barleycorn* is his autobiographical account of his struggles with alcohol. *The People of the Abyss* is a pioneering study of homelessness and poverty on the streets of London, England. In *The Scarlet Plague*, a deadly infection wipes out virtually all of humanity. *The Road* and *The Cruise of the "Snark"* are quite a contrast: the first tells of his adventures as a hobo, the second of his attempt to circle the globe in his own yacht.

Jack London was also an essayist whose interests ranged far and wide. He wrote about surfing in Hawaii, boxing in Australia, the San Francisco Earthquake, politics, driving a horse-drawn wagon through Oregon, wars in Korea and Mexico, sailing, socialism, ranching, dogs, and diseases.

Jack was determined to make his writing realistic and honest. He wanted his readers to see what he had seen, feel what he had felt, imagine what he was imagining. He struggled to make his words clear, his sentences easy to understand. Sometimes this got him in trouble. He was accused during his lifetime of being too violent — some libraries removed his books from the shelves because they thought some of what he had written was too shocking. He was criticized as well for his socialism — for his belief that wealth should be shared, not controlled and hoarded by a few enormously rich companies and individuals.

Today he is sometimes criticized for another reason — racism. Jack grew up at the end of the nineteenth century when openly racist attitudes of white superiority were common in the United States. His own studies of history had convinced him that white Anglo-Saxons were destined to control the world. In some of his stories and novels, the characters we are supposed to like and admire are racists. These stories are difficult to read today because they express attitudes that most people find offensive. Many of these works are no longer in print.

Despite his flaws, it is instructive to see how Jack London achieved all that he did. He was talented, and he was in many ways a visionary, a dreamer. But he was able to realize so many of his dreams and ambitions not because he was a "natural," but because he studied the world's great thinkers, practiced and mastered the details of his craft, and maintained a strenuous daily schedule of reading and writing.

ONE

1876–1887: Boyhood by the Bay

```
I was born in the working class. . . .
My environment was crude and rough and
raw.
```
— Jack London, "What Life Means to Me"

Jack London was not Jack London, not at first. His first name was not originally Jack, nor was his last name London. He was born on January 12, 1876, at 615 Third Street, San Francisco, California, in the home of Amanda Slocum, a friend of his mother. The birth announcement in the *San Francisco Chronicle* on January 13 was simple: "Chaney — In this city, January 12, the wife of W. H. Chaney, of a son." The baby's name was John Griffith Chaney. They called him Johnny.

His mother, Flora Wellman, was born in Massillon, Ohio, in 1843. Her father was a well-to-do businessman who had made a fortune with his warehouse on the Ohio and Erie Canal, which passed through town. During her childhood Flora contracted typhoid fever, which seriously affected her health and appearance for the rest of her life. The disease weakened her eyesight and stunted her growth. It's also possible that the fever forever altered her mental health, for she had numerous emotional problems.

In 1873 she left her family and wandered west, as many people were doing in the mid-nineteenth

The only known photograph of W. H. Chaney, who is probably Jack's father

Flora Wellman, Jack's mother

century. She reappeared in Seattle, Washington, where she met William Henry Chaney.

W. H. Chaney — as he signed his name — was born in Chesterville, Maine, on January 13, 1821. Both of his grandfathers had fought against the British in the American Revolution. As a teenager, Chaney worked at a sawmill, learned the skills of carpentry, and then shipped out on a fishing vessel for two years. Enjoying the life at sea, he enlisted in the Navy. But he hated the military discipline, and so he did what he did throughout his life whenever he found conditions unpleasant: he ran away.

In 1841 Chaney was teaching school in New Orleans. In 1846 he appeared in Wheeling, West Virginia, where he began studying the law and where he made an important discovery about himself — he could write, quickly and easily. He produced a number of stories and novels. But they were never published, and the manuscripts are probably lost forever.

For nine years Chaney's name disappeared from all official records. But in 1866 he resurfaced as an apprentice to Dr. Luke Broughton, a well-known astrologer. In 1869 he headed west — where he met Flora Wellman. She, too, was interested in astrology and in the occult. On June 12, 1874, Chaney married Flora in San Francisco. He apparently did not bother to mention that he was already married at the time — to several different women here and there.

For a while Flora and Chaney enjoyed a business relationship as well as a personal one. Chaney continued to write horoscopes, and Flora conducted séances in their home. She convinced people that she could help them communicate directly with their deceased loved ones. She gave some piano lessons as well.

But when Flora told Chaney that she was pregnant, he reacted in his usual manner when confronted with something he didn't want to face. First he refused to admit he was the father. Then he insisted Flora have an abortion. Finally he said he would abandon her if she delivered the child.

On Friday, June 4, 1875, the *San Francisco Chronicle* printed a shocking story. The headline read: A DISCARDED WIFE. Immediately below this headline, in a fashion popular in the nineteenth century, were two sub-headlines: WHY MRS. CHANEY TWICE ATTEMPTED SUICIDE. And: DRIVEN FROM HOME FOR REFUSING TO DESTROY HER UNBORN INFANT — A CHAPTER OF HEARTLESSNESS AND DOMESTIC MISERY.

Chaney left Flora — and San Francisco — at this time. Not only was he unwilling to support a child, but his astrological business suffered horribly because of the newspaper article. He disappeared from Flora's life forever. She would be but one of his six wives — and a troublesome one, at that.

Now alone and pregnant, Flora moved in with her friends Bill and Amanda Slocum and continued giving séances and piano lessons. But the birth of her son, John Griffith Chaney, was a difficult one, weakening her considerably. She was not able to nurse him, so her physician introduced her to one of his other patients, Daphna Virginia Prentiss, whose child had just died at birth.

Jennie Prentiss, as she was called, was an African-American woman, born on a slave plantation in Tennessee in 1832. In 1867 she married Alonzo Prentiss, a skilled carpenter. Jennie agreed to nurse little Johnny Chaney, who lived with the Prentisses, off and on, for long periods of his childhood. And because Flora was an emotionally cold woman, whose behavior was erratic and unpredictable, Jennie Prentiss became in many ways Jack London's true mother.

In 1875 Flora Chaney met John London, and in September 1876 they married. John London was born into a farming family in Clearfield County, Pennsylvania, on January 11, 1828. Very little is known about his boyhood, but there is a record that he was working as boss of a section gang on a railroad construction project in 1847, and in 1848 he married Anna Jane Cavett. They produced eleven children. Between 1855 and 1860 he was farming in Illinois and Missouri, and on November 9, 1864, he enlisted in the Union Army to fight in the Civil War. Following the war, he moved with his family to the little town of Moscow in

John London, Jack's stepfather, around 1886

eastern Iowa. In 1873 his wife died, leaving John with a huge family he could not care for by himself. No one knows exactly what he did with all the children. He probably placed some with neighbors; others went to orphanages. And he set out with three of them — Charles, Eliza, and Ida — for California. Shortly after they arrived, Charles died, and John placed Ida and Eliza in an orphanage, where they lived for two years until he could once again afford to support them.

When John married Flora Chaney, nine-month-old Johnny Chaney became Johnny London. But it would be twenty years before he would discover that John London was not his biological father.

Johnny spent almost his entire first year of life in the home and care of Jennie and Alonzo Prentiss. He wrote later about some of his earliest memories: a man with gray whiskers carrying him on his shoulder; a feeling of being alone and afraid in the house when he thought the adults had gone; flies buzzing in the window of a warm kitchen.

Throughout his boyhood, he would return from time to time to stay with the Prentisses — especially in times of economic hardship in the London family. It is possible, in fact, that Jennie may have given the little boy the name which the world would know him by — Jack. She confided to a friend that he was such a frisky, energetic child that he reminded her of a jumping jack — so she began calling him "Jackie." The little boy's first words were "Mamma" and "Papa" — but he meant Jennie and Alonzo, not Flora and John London.

Jennie Prentiss would spend hours each day reading to her own young children, William and Priscilla, and to Johnny. She also told them stories she knew from the Bible and stories about her own life, stories told by the old, old people back on the Tennessee plantation where she had lived as a little girl. And when her children brought their schoolbooks home, little Johnny would listen intently as she went over the lessons.

In the first few years of his life, Johnny's parents lived in four different places in San Francisco. In 1879 they moved across the San Francisco Bay to Oakland, where financial circumstances forced them to move again from one small place to another — five in all by 1881. That year John London moved the family to Alameda (near Oakland) where he had bought twenty acres of ranch land. Johnny did not like it. "Life on a California ranch," he wrote later, "was then to me the dullest possible existence. . . ." And on another occasion he complained it was "not very nourishing to the imagination." Nonetheless, for two years the Londons lived on the ranch, raising fruits and vegetables, and Johnny attended school for the first time at the West End School.

On Johnny's seventh birthday (1883), the Londons moved to the Tobin Ranch in San Mateo County, just south of San Francisco, where John London leased seventy-five acres to grow potatoes and raise horses. Johnny entered a country school in San Mateo that he later remembered scornfully. The teacher, London wrote, was an alcoholic, and when he became sufficiently drunk, the older boys in the class — probably thirteen or fourteen years old — would beat him up. The teacher then, to save face, would beat the younger students. "You can think," wrote London, "what sort of school it was."

The nearby Pacific Ocean is spectacularly beautiful along the coast of San Mateo County; tourists today flock to such sites as Half Moon Bay and Grey Whale Cove. But not far inland, where the Londons were trying to make a living from the earth, the landscape was not so interesting to a bright little boy who dreamed of a life of excitement and adventure and whose mind danced with visions of the long ago and faraway.

One of little Johnny's jobs — a dreary one — was to watch the bees and to sound the alarm when they would begin swarming so that the adults could gather them to form honey-producing colonies. The job had one benefit: "I sat under a tree," explained London, "from sunrise till late in the afternoon, waiting for the swarming, [and] I had plenty of time to read and dream."

John London was successful with his leased ranch in San Mateo — by September of 1883, only nine months after they moved there, he had saved enough money to make a down payment on another ranch in the Livermore Valley back on the Oakland side of the San Francisco Bay. Here, the Londons built a barn for horses and invested in chickens. Johnny attended a much better grammar school. And John London was so certain that the family was headed for a comfortable life that he began borrowing more money and investing in neighboring property. By 1885 he had purchased a total of about 125 acres.

It was on this Livermore Valley ranch that Johnny remembered first reading Washington Irving's *Legends of the Alhambra* (tales of medieval Spain) and "Rip Van Winkle." He remembered reading other borrowed books, including a biography of President James A. Garfield and a book about the African travels of Paul Du Chaillu, probably *Explorations and Adventures in Equatorial Africa* (1861).

But Jack London recalled with special fondness a story called *Signa* by a writer named Ouida (whose actual name was Marie Louise de la Ramée). London always claimed that his discovery at the age of eight of a battered copy of this novel had a profound, lasting effect on him — even though the copy he read was missing the final forty pages or so. Over and over and over again he read the story of the little Italian peasant boy who becomes a famous violinist and composer.

In a letter he wrote late in 1911, he declared that the book created his "ambition to get beyond the sky lines of my narrow California valley and opened up to me the possibilities of the world of art. In fact it became my star to which I hitched my child's wagon." It wasn't until 1912 — only a few years before he died — that Jack London found in a secondhand bookshop in Harlem another tattered copy of *Signa*. Eagerly he reread it, learning for the first time the end of the novel.

It was at the ranches that Johnny London first encountered alcohol. In 1913 he published an account of his lifelong struggles with it; he called the book *John Barleycorn*. (Because barley is one of the main ingredients in malt liquors like beer and ale, *John Barleycorn* has for centuries been a slang term for alcohol.) He recalled that the first time he got drunk he was five years old. One of his jobs on the Alameda ranch was to carry a pail full of beer out to his father and the other workers in the field. On one particularly hot day he furtively consumed so much that he staggered alongside his father and the plow horses and remembered sleeping away the rest of the afternoon. "My condition," he wrote, "was like that of one who had gone through a battle with poison. In truth, I had been poisoned."

Two years later — now seven years old and living on the Tobin Ranch in San Mateo — Johnny had another encounter with alcohol. This time it was at a gathering of ranchers and their families. Someone suggested that they all walk four miles to visit a neighboring ranch, and off they went, arriving hot . . . and thirsty. "The red wine was poured in tumblers for all," he wrote. Johnny began drinking his fast, and just as fast his host would refill his glass. Later, drunk, he staggered toward a nearby bridge, where he fell fast asleep on his back.

Despite getting horribly sick from that experience, he fondly remembered the thrill of going with his father into a saloon — "a delightful and desirable place," he wrote. While the men drank — and seemed to have such a wonderful time doing so — he got to warm himself by the stove and eat a free soda cracker. He remembered one bartender who mixed for him a drink of sweet syrup and soda water, and this man became, he wrote, "my ideal of a good, kind man." These were powerful images forming in the highly impressionable mind of a very young boy. It would take years for Jack London to come out on top in his lifelong wrestling match with John Barleycorn.

On the Livermore Ranch, things went well for a

while. But then the money began to run short once again; to Flora, there just never seemed to be enough. She decided to take in boarders and invited Captain James Shepard, a forty-year-old widower with three children, to come live with them. This meant an extra burden on Johnny's stepsister Eliza, now a teenager. Not only did she have to look after Johnny, but now there were three other children in the household as well. But Eliza was soon captivated by Shepard, who was a Civil War veteran, and in 1885, when she was only about eighteen, she married the much older man and moved with his family to Oakland.

Flora, meanwhile, had determined that they ought to invest more heavily in chickens — surely the sale of eggs and poultry would turn a steady profit. But no sooner had they bought all the birds than an epidemic wiped out the entire flock, virtually bankrupting the Londons. They lost the ranch when they could not meet their payments. Once again, they had to move.

Back in Oakland, the Londons used their little remaining cash to buy a small home only two blocks from the Shepards. For extra cash, they took in boarders — usually young women who were working at a nearby cotton mill. But money remained a problem. Flora did not improve their situation by spending much of their loose cash on the Chinese lottery, a daily numbers game operated by the Chinese immigrants in the San Francisco Bay area.

Jack, age ten, and his dog Rollo

Now ten years old, Johnny London began earning money for the family — a burden he would bear for the rest of his life. His first job — selling and delivering newspapers on the streets of Oakland — brought in three dollars a month. But he also made a wonderful discovery: the Oakland Public Library. The library was an old, two-story wooden building. On the first floor were newspapers and magazines. On the second — where Johnny loved to go — were the fiction and reference books. On one wall the shelves reached to the ceiling.

Johnny could not believe that he could actually enter this building full of books and remove from

City Hall in Oakland, California; the Oakland Public Library is at left

it — at no cost! — all he wanted to read. And he wanted to read everything. He charged into that building every day, "eagerly reading," he wrote later, "everything that came to my hand." In *John Barleycorn* he remembered that he read "principally history and adventure, and all the old travels and voyages." He remembered that he spent entire days reading. "I read in bed, I read at table, I read as I walked to and from school, and I read at recess while the other boys were playing." Jack London never lost these habits of voracious reading. And it was not until he became a successful writer, he said, and was able to buy books for himself that he finally stopped his regular visits to the Oakland Public Library.

But reading everything is not an efficient — or practical — way to proceed in a library. Fortunately for Johnny London, in Oakland there was a wonderful librarian, Ina Coolbrith, who encouraged the ten-year-old and began to direct his reading. When he was thirty years old and already a world-famous writer, Jack London wrote a letter to her, thanking her for all she had done for him. He called her "a goddess."

The Londons continued moving from house to

Ina Coolbrith, librarian at the Oakland Public Library

house in the Oakland area throughout Johnny's boyhood. They moved four times in 1887, Johnny's eleventh year, and in the spring of that year they were living in West Oakland. Johnny was glad that the Prentiss family lived nearby — they, too, were moving around during these years. Alonzo and Jennie were always glad to see him, always welcomed him into their home as if he were a member of their family.

While the Londons were living in West Oakland, Johnny attended Cole Grammar School, along with Priscilla Prentiss, who was three years older. Cole was a very large, two-story, wooden-frame structure surrounded by an iron fence. It was Victorian in design, and resembled a very large house with high ceilings and tall windows that let in lots of California sunlight. Through them, no doubt, Johnny London stared at the distant hills where he longed to roam.

At Cole, Johnny was a superior student, and he also made a lifelong friend, Frank Atherton. In later years, Atherton wrote a book (never published) about his experiences with Jack London. He called it *Jack London in Boyhood Adventures,* and although it sometimes exaggerates events, it contains some valuable information about Johnny London's life in school and on the streets of Oakland.

One day while the boys were in school, there was an explosion at a nearby factory; Cole Grammar School, wrote Frank, shook "like a gigantic rattle box." Glass shattered, plaster fell from the ceiling and shuddered off the walls, powdering desks and children.

Jack's class at Cole Grammar School (Jack is circled);
his friend Frank Atherton is third from left in the third row.

Desperate students and teachers abandoned all order
and stampeded for the exits; some fell and were tram-
pled by the others. It was madness. Outside, Johnny
proudly announced to Frank that he'd brought something out with him — a library book.

Frank also remembered that Johnny had a Sunday
job setting up pins in a neighborhood bowling alley.
But when his father was off on Sundays, they would go
fishing, either out in the Bay on a rented rowboat, or
out on the ferryboat wharf.

One Saturday, Frank stopped by the Londons'
house while Flora was in the middle of conducting a
séance. Johnny explained to his friend that Flora believed that during her séances she was possessed by the
spirit of an American Indian chief named Plume. Peo-

ple paid Flora to have Plume contact other spirits, usually dead relatives or friends. Frank could hear "strange,
weird moanings" coming from the London house as
Flora/Plume delivered messages from the spirit world to
the paying customers.

Johnny London and Frank Atherton graduated
from the Cole Grammar School in 1887. For Johnny,
age eleven, this was the end of his schooling for about
eight years. Like many other children from families
who were not well-off, he now had to go to work to help
earn his keep. In one way, his boyhood — what little of
it he had — was over. Now he would become a la-
borer — a member of the great working class whose
lives he later tried to improve through his writing.

TWO

1888–1893: Sailor Jack — Pirate and Patrolman

From the time I was twelve, I listened to the lure of the sea.
— Jack London, "The Joy of Small-Boat Sailing"

Both 1888 and 1889 were years of change as well as years of dreary sameness for Johnny London. The family moved, of course. After the little bungalow on Seventh Street in Oakland, they rented a five-room house on Pine Street, which is very near the waterfront. And Johnny's daily routine continued — delivering newspapers and picking up other jobs where he could.

During his teenage years the streets of Oakland were occasionally mean streets. Johnny, however, was able to defend himself with his fists when necessary. He later recalled with pride how he had once defeated three brothers, one after the other, who had been bothering him on his paper route.

In 1891, at age fifteen, Johnny went to work for the R. Hickmott Canning Company in Oakland, a company that packaged fruits and vegetables. Johnny operated a machine that filled, closed, and then soldered shut the cans. It was a boring, mind-numbing job that greatly depressed this boy with the wide imagination and dreams of distant places. The pay was ten cents per

807 Pine Street, in West Oakland, where Jack lived from 1888 to 1890

hour. He was at work by six in the morning and had only a half-hour lunch break, then another half hour for supper. "I worked every night till ten, eleven and twelve o'clock." He made no more than fifty dollars per month, nearly all of which he turned over to Flora for household expenses . . . and the lottery.

Johnny was trying to save money for a skiff — a small, one-person sailboat. In the 1890s the San Francisco Bay was thick with sailing vessels. The masts of hundreds of ships rose like leafless trees along the waterfront. Ships were an important means of transportation. They carried goods all over the world. And many young people like Johnny dreamed of going to sea. It would be an escape, they thought, from a dull, landlocked life.

He had found a skiff for sale for eight dollars. After months of effort and self-denial — he worked one shift that lasted thirty-six hours — he had managed to set aside about five dollars. Then, he recalled, Flora showed up unexpectedly at the factory one day. "My mother came to the machine where I worked and asked for it. I could have killed myself that night. After a year of hell . . . to be robbed of that petty joy."

He contented himself, for the present, with using his father's skiff — a fourteen-footer with a centerboard that he sailed around the bay. Johnny acquired sailing skills by listening, by watching, and by simply getting out on the water with his father on fishing expeditions and practicing.

One expert who was especially helpful was William Shorey, a whaling captain who was an acquaintance of Jennie and Alonzo Prentiss. When he was in port, he kept an eye on Johnny, for the bay was dangerous. The water was frigid, winds and storms were always unpredictable, currents were tricky, and sharks were always waiting below to feed on the careless or the unlucky.

Johnny eventually became a highly skilled small-boat sailor. His second wife, Charmian, wrote later that he was at his happiest when sailing — "Dawn or twilight, he loved the way of a boat upon the sea." His daughter Joan believed that the skiff was his escape from his grim life in the cannery. "Alone in his small boat," she wrote, "he was master, not slave. He could go where he wished . . . or he could lie back, day-dreaming . . . or watching the wild ducks flying against the sunset-stained sky."

One of the waterfront characters Johnny London met during these years was "French Frank," one of a group of men known around the bay as "oyster pirates." At night they would rob the oyster beds owned by the commercial fishing companies, then sell the shellfish in the morning to restaurants and saloons.

One day Johnny learned that French Frank wanted to sell his sloop, the *Razzle Dazzle*, for the staggering price of three hundred dollars. But Johnny was excited. If he could somehow find the money, he would have a boat of his own — and a crew member. With the boat would come a twenty-year-old hand named "Spider" Healey, whom Jack later described as a "black-whiskered wharf-rat." Among the waterfront crowd Johnny would then become an equal, a man among men. He borrowed the money from Jennie Prentiss, promising to pay it back with his earnings from the vessel.

The deal for the transfer of the *Razzle Dazzle* was closed in a place that still stands on Oakland's waterfront and in fact looks much as it did then — Johnny Heinold's First and Last Chance Saloon. The small structure was originally built in 1880 from the ruins of an old whaling ship. Johnny Heinold bought the building in 1883 and remained the owner-bartender for

Johnny Heinold, Jack's friend and the owner of an Oakland waterfront saloon

fifty years. He would be a friend to Jack London all his life.

Johnny had some exciting moments aboard the *Razzle Dazzle*. He wrote with pride about bringing in "a bigger load of oysters than any other two-man team"; he boasted about a race among the pirates, about how he arrived "first of the fleet," which meant he would make the best sales that day.

But it was not long before Johnny became bored with his life as an oyster pirate. He was not making the money he thought he would — and the little money he did make was disappearing in the First and Last Chance Saloon. He was not repaying Jennie Prentiss on the schedule he had promised.

And even worse: after several months there was an accidental fire aboard the *Razzle Dazzle*, destroying the mainsail, so Johnny could not use the vessel. After an argument with some of his partners, he decided to abandon his ship and join "Old Scratch" Nelson, another pirate, aboard his ship, the *Reindeer*. Old Scratch had earned his name in his many waterfront fights. It was said he would scratch off the face of an opponent.

But this life soon lost its appeal as well. He was no longer captain of his own boat; instead, he was taking orders. Johnny felt his life was not headed anywhere. Then came an offer to join the Fish Patrol. Formed in 1883, the Fish Patrol was responsible for controlling the very kinds of illegal activities that Johnny and his companions were involved in. He would be a "deputy patrolman," which meant he would earn money not from a salary but from a percentage of the fines paid by the lawbreakers he was able to round up. And so he set out helping the Fish Patrol arrest the very men he had been competing with for months.

His daughter Joan wrote later that he did this not out of a desire to see law and order enforced — and not because he wished to betray his waterfront acquaintances. "To earn a living," she wrote, "and to maintain his independence of time clocks and long hours at a machine, to know still more of the life on the San Francisco Bay, to satisfy his delight in sailing — these were the factors involved."

Johnny had many adventures on the Bay while sailing with the oyster pirates and the Fish Patrol, and a number of them appear in two books he later wrote, *The Cruise of the "Dazzler"* (1902) and *Tales of the Fish Patrol* (1905).

Dazzler is a short novel about a teenage character named Joe Bronson who lives in San Francisco. He is a bored student who loves to fight and live roughly on the streets. After he fails some exams at school, he runs away to work aboard the *Dazzler* because his disappointed father threatens to send him to military school. He discovers to his surprise that the vessel is not like the romantic ships he had read about in books. Instead, it is a pirate ship run by French Pete and 'Frisco Kid, a boy about Joe's age. They fail in their first theft, then are caught in a storm and join another vessel, the *Reindeer,* whose crew is plotting to steal a safe from a business onshore. Joe is stunned to learn that it is his father's business they are planning to rob. But a storm interferes with the plans, sinking the *Reindeer.* Joe and 'Frisco Kid drift in on the tide in the damaged *Dazzler* and return the safe. 'Frisco hops a train out of town. But Joe arranges for him to get a $2,500 reward and the opportunity to receive an education.

Tales of the Fish Patrol is a collection of seven stories, loosely connected by a sixteen-year-old character named Jack and his companion, Charley Le Grant. One typical story is "A Raid on the Oyster Pirates." Jack and Charley acquire a nearly wrecked ship and pretend to join the oyster pirates. While the pirates are out on a shoal raiding an oyster bed, Jack and Charley take their boats, leaving the pirates stranded to face the rising tide. As the water rises, threatening to drown the pirates, they surrender to the young patrolmen. In a 1903 letter to *Youth's Companion,* a magazine that published his *Fish Patrol* stories, London explained that the collection was based on fact. "The oyster bed raid I have described in one of the stories," he wrote, "is almost literally a narrative of an actual raid."

When Johnny was only sixteen and working for the Fish Patrol, alcohol very nearly killed him. He had sailed up to Benicia, California, near the Carquinez Straits, where San Pablo Bay narrows to a mere two miles. For three weeks he had been drinking steadily. About one o'clock one morning, totally drunk, he was attempting to step from the wharf onto the deck of a boat. He slipped and fell into the water, where the full force of the tide swept him away.

At first he was not worried — he was a strong swimmer, and the evening was pleasant. He removed his clothes and floated on the tide. Soon, time and the chill of the water began to sober him, but by then he was weak and nearly numb with the cold, and the current was powerful. After four hours in the water, he was very near death. And then . . . a miracle. A passing fisherman spotted Johnny in the water and pulled him aboard.

During Johnny's oyster pirate and Fish Patrol days, the Londons continued to move their household from one Oakland address to another. In 1891 and 1892, they were living on Eighth Street, then on West Street, then on Park Way. There they occupied a small home that had been constructed of materials from other dismantled buildings — including the bowling alley where Johnny had once been a pin-setter.

When he left the Fish Patrol in 1892 and returned to live ashore, he was sixteen years old, had very little education, suffered from a severe drinking problem, and appeared to have a dreary and hopeless future. If he continued this way of life, it was doubtful that he would survive his teenage years.

He was not helping his family any longer. He was living on the waterfront and on the streets, running with a rough group of young men. "I practically lived in saloons; became a barroom loafer, and worse," he wrote later. On one of his sailing trips up into the Suisun Bay he and a companion named Nickey decided to sail on up to Sacramento on the river of the same name. At a sandbar near a railroad bridge, the boys went swimming and met a group of "road-kids" — homeless teenagers who hopped trains for thrills. To be considered one of them, newcomers had to make it over the mountains into Nevada — and back — without being caught by the railroad authorities.

These boys greatly impressed Johnny. They made his oyster-pirating "look like thirty cents," he wrote. He decided to join them. "I was just as strong as any of them," he remembered, "just as quick, just as nervy, and my brain was just as good." While he was among them for a couple of weeks, he received a moniker — or nickname (a "monica," as he called it): "Sailor Kid" or "'Frisco Jack."

In the evening they went out in the streets of Sacramento, begging for money. At first, he was disgusted by this — it was beneath his dignity. But when he saw how much fun the road-kids were having, his attitude soon changed. He came to see begging as "a joyous prank, a game of wits, a nerve-exerciser."

A few days later Sailor Kid had to prove himself by riding over the mountains and back. He leaped aboard a moving mail car and climbed to the roof, where he lay flat. Later, he learned that "French Kid," a young runaway from San Francisco who had tried to hop the same train, had lost both his legs in the attempt. But Johnny made the round-trip safely across and was then, officially, a road-kid.

Later, Jack London admitted that at times the road-kids were dangerous. They would occasionally rob people in the streets — especially drunks and lone pedestrians. They could be like wolves, he wrote, and "like wolves they are capable of dragging down the strongest man. . . . They will fling themselves upon a man and hold on with every ounce of strength in their wiry bodies, till he is thrown and helpless."

Back in Oakland, he once again found Old Scratch Nelson, a companion from the oyster pirate days, and began living a rough, violent life on the streets and waterfront — and in the saloons, especially Heinold's. He worked odd jobs occasionally, but for the most part he lived a wild, undisciplined life. "I became pretty thoroughly alcohol-soaked during this period," he wrote.

During the winter of 1892, sailors from the seal-hunting fleet were ashore in San Francisco and Oakland. In the saloons on both sides of the Bay, Johnny began to associate with some of these hunters and decided that when the fleet sailed, he would go with them. "The adventure-lust was strong in me," he wrote

later. And on January 12, 1893 — his seventeenth birthday — he left California aboard the *Sophia Sutherland*, a
three-masted schooner, for a seven-month seal-hunting
voyage to the Sea of Japan.

Native peoples in the North had hunted seals for
centuries, wasting little of the animal in the process.
But the sealing fleet that Johnny London sailed with
was interested in hides only. They wanted skins only
from the females or adolescent seals, for the hides of
older males often bore the scars of battle.

The first week brought Johnny his first physical
test among the rough and violent men aboard the ship.
While he was weaving a mat, a large sailor accused
him — falsely — of eating too much of the molasses
and ordered him to refill the container. Johnny refused.
The sailor threatened Johnny, and when the youth re-

The Sophia Sutherland

fused once again, the older man prepared to punch Johnny into obedience. He never got the chance. Johnny slugged the sailor between the eyes, and the battle was on. When the sailor charged, Johnny dodged, leaping to the larger man's back and choking him from behind. The sailor jumped up and down, slamming Johnny into the low ceiling of the ship, but the youth held fast, and soon the older man's face turned purple and he was nearly unconscious. Finally, he gasped that he would leave Johnny alone.

Johnny had learned that in fights with grown men he must strike quickly or lose. And so aboard the *Sophia Sutherland* he exploded into action at the first hint of trouble. "I might be beaten in the subsequent fight," he wrote, "but I left the impression that I was a wild-cat and that I would just as willingly fight again."

For fifty-one days after they passed through the Golden Gate, the *Sophia Sutherland* was in the open ocean, and Johnny was living a life he had always dreamed of. He was a deep-sea sailor, on a hunting voyage with men. They were pursuing large, intelligent animals that fled before them, not simple oysters that lay there, helpless, waiting to be picked up. He had learned how to get along aboard the ship — work hard and fight harder. He was experiencing life, he thought, the way it really was. He had even witnessed a death and a burial at sea — of a brutal sailor known only as "the Bricklayer." This man, wrote Jack, was "one of those horrible monstrous things that one must see in order to be convinced that they exist." After the burial, Johnny took the Bricklayer's bunk — something his superstitious shipmates warned him never to do. But Johnny insisted. And later that night — on watch — he swore he saw the ghost of the Bricklayer floating on the surface of the midnight sea. It terrified Johnny. Later he discovered it had been only the moonlit shadow of the topmast.

Johnny was grateful there was no alcohol aboard the ship, and as the days passed, his system cleansed itself. He grew stronger with the daily labor. Among his shipmates he saw men who had been thoroughly broken by alcohol. A man named Louis, for example, had lost to alcohol all his "power and place and comfort"; he was a man without pride, without a future. Johnny looked at Louis and hoped he was not looking in a mirror.

In the Bonin Islands — five hundred miles south of Tokyo, Japan — Johnny finally had the opportunity to go ashore. He joined two shipmates, Victor and Axel, in a little town where they found hundreds of other sailors from other ships. They decided to stop into a saloon before exploring the island. They never really left that saloon. There, for ten days, they drank and fought and howled and rioted in the streets. One morning Johnny woke up on one of the streets and discovered he was missing his money, watch, coat, belt, and shoes.

Finally, the *Sophia Sutherland* headed northward once again, and for one hundred days they hunted seals — "wild and heavy work," he later called

Jack, age 17, on his 1893 seal-hunting voyage aboard the Sophia Sutherland

it — chasing the animals in open boats, harpooning them as they swam desperately to escape. In his novel *The Sea-Wolf* he provides some detail about the hunt — and its aftermath:

> After a good day's killing I have seen our decks covered with hides and bodies,

slippery with fat and blood, the scuppers
[drains on the deck] running red; masts,
ropes, and rails spattered with the san-
guinary [bloody] color; and the men, like
butchers plying their trade, naked and
red of arm and hand, hard at work with
ripping and flensing-knives [skinning
knives], removing the skins from the
pretty sea-creatures they had killed.

It was my task to tally the pelts as
they came aboard from the boats, to
oversee the skinning and afterward the
cleansing of the decks and bringing
things shipshape again. It was not
pleasant work. My soul and my stomach
revolted at it. . . .

When the hold of the ship was finally stuffed with
hides, the *Sophia Sutherland* sailed south to Yokohama,
Japan, where they would sell their catch. For two weeks
Johnny saw little but the insides of saloons. From Yokohama they soon sailed for San Francisco. The sailors
were paid their final wage, then stormed ashore . . . and
into the first saloon they saw, its open doors beckoning
them inside for one last friendly drink before they
parted company.

Nearly all of the nineteen men who went into
that saloon with Johnny London drank up all their
wages, and in a few days, their money gone, they sailed
out on other ships. But Johnny headed across the Bay
to Oakland before all of his disappeared. In a bitter letter he told what happened to the rest of his pay: "I

bought a second hand hat, some forty-cent shirts, two fifty-cent suits of underclothes, and a second hand coat and vest. . . . The rest went to pay the debts of my father and to the family."

Back in Oakland, he found that much had changed in the seven months he had been away. Some comrades from the oyster pirate days were dead or in jail. Others had simply vanished, leaving no clue to their whereabouts. Another had killed two men and fled the authorities. A friend from the Fish Patrol had died after being stabbed in the lung. Once again, in these deaths and disappearances and imprisonments of men he had known, Johnny London glimpsed the grim face of his own dim future.

But Johnny did not return to a life in Oakland that seemed any more promising than when he had left. The American economy was not doing well, and there simply were not many high-paying jobs available for people who had only a grade-school education. But his family needed whatever money he could bring in. His mother told him that he should stop his wandering — it was time to settle down and find a regular job. So once again, he picked up whatever employment he could find, working long, difficult hours at tedious tasks that demanded little of this bright, energetic young man now nearing his eighteenth birthday.

His first job was in a jute mill — perhaps the Pacific Jute Manufacturing Company in Oakland. (Jute is a coarse fiber used to make material like burlap.) Johnny's job — at the going rate of ten cents per hour — was to operate a machine that would wind the twine made from the jute.

He tried to stop drinking during this period of his life, even attending events at the Young Men's Christian Association (Y.M.C.A.). But he did not feel he really belonged there: "The life there was healthful and athletic," he wrote, "but too juvenile." Because he had known "mysterious and violent things," he thought, he "possessed a sadder and more terrible wisdom" that set him forever apart from other young men his age.

He did make a new friend — Louis Shattuck, a youth from the neighborhood who worked in a blacksmith shop. Louis, remembered Jack, was "handsome, and graceful, and filled with love for the girls." But both of them had trouble developing any social life — or any contacts with young women — because their spending money for the week usually never exceeded a dollar apiece.

The best they could do was to walk around the streets in the early evening and look for groups of young women doing the same thing. But Johnny felt uncomfortable and shy around women. "They were strange and wonderful to me," he said, "after my precocious man's life. I failed of the bold front and the necessary forwardness when the crucial moment came."

In *John Barleycorn*, London wrote about a young woman he called "Haydee." He met her at a Salvation Army meeting. For a half hour they sat, side by side, neither speaking. On the other side of Haydee sat her aunt, chaperoning. Johnny was entranced by the young woman: "She had a slender oval face," he recalled. "Her brown eyes were beautiful." He eventually mustered the courage to speak to her, and they had a few dates. But nothing further developed. Nonetheless, she remained in his mind, his first love. "I know I loved her; and I dreamed day dreams of her for a year and more," he wrote, "and the memory of her is very dear."

Then Louis and Johnny began going to the National Saloon, spending their money on alcohol. Now they no longer had even the few cents they needed to associate with the respectable young women of Oakland.

When the jute mill did not come through with a promised raise for Johnny — amounting to about twenty-five cents per day — he abruptly quit. But not before he had his first public success as a writer. London remembered from his days in school that he had "written the usual compositions which had been praised in the usual way," and while he was working in the jute mill, he decided to make "an occasional try" at writing.

Years later, his wife Charmian wrote that it was his mother who first noticed in the San Francisco *Morning Call* a contest for the best descriptive article by writers under age twenty-two, and it was his mother who suggested he write about one of his experiences on the seal-hunting voyage. He thought about the idea for a few moments, wrote Charmian. "All at once, with a grin, he swooped down upon the kitchen table with an old school tablet, where he wrote furiously without note of the clock until breakfast." For two more nights he worked on the piece, reducing it to the two-thousand-word limit set by the newspaper. Then Flora carried the manuscript across the San Francisco Bay to the newspaper offices and handed it to the editor.

The story — Jack London's first published work — was called "Story of a Typhoon off the Coast of Japan." It appeared on November 12, 1893, under the name *John London*. He won the twenty-five-dollar first prize — practically a month's salary at the jute mill. And he was especially pleased to learn that the second- and third-place winners were college students, one from Stanford University, the other from the University of California at Berkeley. John London, of Cole Grammar School, had defeated them both. His father was so proud he bought every copy of the *Morning Call* he could afford to give to his friends.

"Story of a Typhoon off the Coast of Japan" is clearly a story written by an amateur, but it shows flashes of the talent that would one day make the name *Jack London* known to readers all over the world. One of the early paragraphs reveals London's abilities, even at seventeen, to paint a scene for readers: "Away off to the northward Cape Jerimo reared its black, forbidding head like some huge monster rising from the deep. The winter's snow, not yet entirely dissipated by the sun, covered it in patches of glistening white, over which the light wind swept on its way out to sea. Huge gulls rose slowly, fluttering their wings in the light breeze and striking their webbed feet on the surface of the water for over half a mile before they could leave it."

But despite this early success, London's literary career did not immediately begin after "Typhoon." As he wrote later, he felt his "blood was still too hot for a settled routine," and he tried to publish in the *Call* only one more time during this period (the newspaper quickly rejected the piece).

When Johnny left the jute mill, there were still not many career opportunities available to him. But as he looked around the city, he noticed an increasing use of electricity. And so he went to the power plant owned and operated by one of the city's streetcar lines — the Oakland, San Leandro, and Haywards Electric Railway. He told the manager he wanted to learn to be an electrician. The manager encouraged Johnny, but said he must first prove himself as a shoveler of coal, the fuel that powered the electric generators for the streetcars. For thirty dollars per month, he would work ten-hour days, including Sundays, with a one-day vacation per month.

He quickly learned that completing his work in ten hours was impossible. "I never finished my task before eight at night," he wrote; instead, he worked twelve to thirteen hours a day — and was not paid for his overtime. When he left work late that first night, he boarded the streetcar for his three-mile ride home. When the car neared his stop, he found he could barely stand up: his stiffened muscles refused to cooperate. He staggered home and fell asleep at the kitchen table before his mother could even bring his supper to him. Flora and John carried him — like a giant baby — to his room, where they undressed him and put him to bed.

And so his dreary life dragged on. He had no more time for books, for dates with girls. "I was a proper work-beast," he wrote. "I worked, and ate, and slept, while my mind slept all the time. The whole thing was a nightmare." Then one day one of the other workers took him aside and told him that he had been doing the work of two men, who had each been paid forty dollars per month.

Disgusted, he went immediately home, he remembered, "and proceeded to sleep the clock around." And when he finally awoke, he had no job and no plans. The strain of all the shoveling had weakened his wrists so severely that for a year afterward he had to wear supporting leather straps around them.

The thought of working any longer was "repulsive," he wrote later. "Learning a trade could go hang." And so he resolved to travel again — though not by sea. This time he would return to the life he had briefly sampled with the road-kids in Sacramento. "So I headed out on the adventure-path again," he said, "starting to tramp East by beating my way on the railroads." He did not know at the time, of course, that he would be staying in Buffalo for a month as a guest of the state of New York at the Erie County Penitentiary.

THREE

1894: On the Road Again

```
I became a tramp — well, because of the
life that was in me, of the wanderlust
in my blood that would not let me rest.
```
— Jack London, *The Road*

Johnny London was one of the millions who were un-employed in the United States in 1894. Farm prices were low, forcing layoffs of workers in agriculture. Banks were taking back land from people who could not make the payments on their loans. Businesses of all sorts were failing. Financial markets on Wall Street were reeling. And there was no "safety net" of welfare or public assistance to help those who had lost their jobs and homes and farms and businesses.

Jacob Coxey, a political activist, was organizing what he hoped would be a huge march to protest un-employment in the United States. He believed that one solution was for the government to provide con-struction projects — and jobs. If Congress would pay for new bridges and roads and dams, the unemployed workers of America would build them. The march began, coincidentally, in Flora London's hometown, Massil-lon, Ohio. The marchers left in a snowstorm, heading for Washington, D. C., where "General Coxey's Army of the Unemployed" hoped to gain attention, earn public sympathy, and put pressure on Congress to do something about this worsening problem.

Coxey had arranged for a handful of other "armies" from around the nation to join his in Washington. In Oakland, Charles T. Kelly, a local printer and labor organizer, began to enlist marchers from the Bay Area for the big demonstration. Many in the community were opposed to the demonstrators — calling them "bums" and "hoboes" and blaming them for unsolved crimes in the area. But Johnny London, fresh from quitting the jute mill, decided to join them. His parents were not excited about his decision, but they did not try to stop him. His stepsister Eliza privately gave him a ten-dollar gold piece she had saved.

The organizers had arranged — or so they thought — for the demonstrators to receive free rail transportation for at least part of their journey. But on Friday, April 6, 1894, the day Johnny planned to leave with Kelly's Army, he was asleep at home when the other marchers, camped near the railroad yards, were rounded up by the police and some angry citizens and put on an earlier train. When Johnny arrived at the depot that morning at the arranged time, he and many others found that the army of approximately seven hundred had left them behind.

Johnny was not discouraged. Using some of Eliza's money, he bought a ticket for a later train to Sacramento, about eighty miles away. But when he arrived, he found that General Kelly's Army had already continued eastward into Utah several hours before. Not wishing to spend any more of the little money he had with him, Johnny decided to use the skills he had learned from the road-kids a year before: he would board and ride the trains illegally. It would not take him long to catch the army.

Johnny was not traveling alone. A friend from Oakland, Frank Davis, was with him. But after a few days of dodging the authorities, of clinging to fast-moving railroad cars, of suffering bitter cold in the mountains, Frank Davis decided to return home. Johnny was not angry or disappointed. We know this because of something Frank gave him before he left: a small address book, five by seven inches in size. Johnny used it to record some brief notes about his experiences heading east. This "tramp diary" contains about sixty-five pages of London's handwritten notes — a sign that Johnny was more seriously considering writing as a career.

In the diary entry for Wednesday, April 11, 1894, London wrote about Frank's decision to go home: "This afternoon Frank and I had an understanding. The road has no more charms for him. The romance and adventure are gone and nothing remains but the stern reality of the hardships to be endured. Though he has decided to turn west again I am sure the experience has done him good, broadened his thoughts, given a better understanding of the low strata of society and surely will have made him more charitable to the tramps he will meet hereafter when he is in better circumstances."

In the diary Johnny recorded a number of incidents on his journey east:

- While holding on to a train in Nevada, he smelled something burning: "A spark caught fire in my overcoat and [was] smoldering away [and] suddenly burst into flames. The train was going about forty miles an hour and it was quite a job to put it out. My overcoat and coat were ruined."

- *Thursday, April 19*: In western Iowa, he finally caught up with Kelly's Army. London wrote elsewhere about the impressive sight: "General Kelly sat a magnificent black charger, and with waving banners, to the martial music of fife and drum corps, company by company, in two divisions, his two thousand stiffs [tramps] countermarched before him. . . ."

- *Tuesday, April 24*: The army was making slow progress through Iowa. In an essay, "Two Thousand Stiffs" (1907), London remembered how well the people treated the marchers: "They turned out with their wagons and carried our baggage; gave us hot lunches at noon by the wayside; . . . and the good citizens turned out by the hundreds, locked arms, and marched with us down their main streets. It was circus day when we came to town, and every day was circus day, for there were many towns."

- *Tuesday, May 1–Sunday, May 6*: Because the railroad would no longer provide transportation, the army leadership decided to build flatboats to float down the Des Moines River to the Mississippi and to the Ohio — an itinerary that would get the army close to Washing-

With Kelly's Army in 1894; Jack grins at the camera in the lower right corner

ton. Johnny's nautical skills came in very handy from here on — he made sure his boat stayed at the front. By arriving at the destinations first, Johnny and his party were assured of the best campsites and supplies. They collected for themselves the small portions of tobacco, sugar, and coffee that kindly farmers and townspeople had left for the army leaders.

• *Thursday, May 24–Friday, May 25*: Johnny and some friends decided to leave General Kelly's Army. "I can't stand starvation," he wrote in his diary. They continued eastward by hopping trains.

• *Tuesday, May 29*: Johnny arrived in Chicago, where he found nine letters waiting for him at the post office. One from his mother contained four dollars — a fortune for a young man who had been penniless for weeks. She wrote: "John, under no circumstances place yourself in a position to be imprisoned; you have gone to see the country and not to spend your time behind bars." That night he paid fifteen cents for a bed — "the first bed I had lain in since leaving home," he commented in his diary.

• *Wednesday, May 30, 1894*: Johnny arrived at the fairgrounds of the World's Columbian Exposition — also known as the World's Fair — in Chicago. Only a few months before the grounds of the fair had been a spectacular display of modern engineering and architecture, but by the time he visited, the exhibits were all gone, and hundreds of homeless people were living in the ruins of what only months before had been beautiful, gleaming white buildings.

• *Thursday, May 31, 1894*: Johnny took the steamer *City of Chicago* across Lake Michigan to St. Joseph, Michigan. He was going to visit his mother's sister, Mary Everhard. This is the final entry in the "tramp diary." Johnny spent several weeks with the Everhards, resting, eating, and being somewhat spoiled by the attention of these relatives he had never met.

But one morning he arose knowing it was time to leave. He bid his family good-bye and hopped yet another eastbound train, this time for Buffalo, New York, where he planned to see one of nature's greatest displays, Niagara Falls. But he spent only one evening viewing the falls; he spent the following thirty days in prison.

After his experiences on the *Sophia Sutherland,* on the road, in the devastated White City of the World's Fair, and now in the Erie County Penitentiary, he had certainly seen the underside of life. He was slipping lower and lower down the ladder of life. But he had not reached the bottom rung.

After his release from prison in late July 1894, he once again hopped a train, this time heading southeast to Washington, D. C. He visited all the important monuments and buildings and memorials in the city — though he was disappointed in the coldness of the people there. He had a difficult time begging for food and money in the nation's capital. But he found a job in a stable. In return for taking care of a few horses in the morning, he was given a blanket and allowed to sleep in one of the stalls.

One night he returned to the stable about nine o'clock and found a game of dice going on among some of the other stable workers. As he stood watching, he suddenly heard a commotion at the doors. It was a police raid. Officers swarmed into the stable, swinging their clubs wildly, grabbing prisoners. Johnny remembered that he "ducked a swat from a club, dived between a bull's [policeman's] legs, and was free. And then how I ran!"

This seemed like a good time to leave the city. He caught a train for Baltimore, where he stayed a few days. He was fascinated by Druid Hill Park. Here was a public place where men — "educated hoboes," his

daughter called them — gave speeches about economics, about society, about the unfairness of a political
system that permitted some people to be enormously
rich while others had nothing at all. Listening to these
men, Johnny began to realize how little he knew about
history, economics, philosophy, science, and sociology.
He felt he was unable to participate and compete in this
sort of intellectual free-for-all that he found so exciting — even when he spent hours in the Baltimore public library trying to dig out information to use in his
debates and discussions. He resolved to go home.

He headed north to Montreal. From there he
would once again turn his face to the west, clear across
Canada, and home. His first stop on the way north was
New York City. The activity and life in the city excited
him greatly, and he must have been dazzled by the sight
of the Brooklyn Bridge, which had been completed
only about ten years earlier and was considered an ar-
chitectural wonder of the world. Yet on the streets —
especially in the Bowery section of the city where there
were many cheap hotels and saloons — he once again
saw the hungry, desperate faces of the poor and the
homeless, the people at the bottom of the social ladder — the ones who lived in what he later called "the
Social Pit."

It was very hot during the time he was in New
York City. In the mornings he would walk around to see
the sights, but in the afternoons he would relax in a little park near City Hall. Men with pushcarts would sell
damaged books for a few pennies each, and there were

booths where Johnny would buy ice-cold milk for a penny a glass. It was so hot he drank ten to fifteen glasses each afternoon.

One day he noticed a crowd forming in the park. As he moved closer, he discovered they were watching a game of "pee-wee" (marbles) — a game outlawed on the streets of New York. Just then someone yelled, "Bull!" The marble-players ran, but Johnny didn't. He did not know at the time that the game was illegal. As a policeman approached him casually, he stood there, watching, never dreaming that he was the one the officer was after. Johnny learned soon enough. "Bang! His club came down on top of my head, and I was reeling backward like a drunken man, the curious faces of the onlookers billowing up and down like the waves of the sea, my precious book falling from under my arm into the dirt, the bull advancing with the club ready for another blow." Johnny had a vision at that moment: he saw himself, bloody-headed, standing in a police court. He knew what would follow — jail. He ran and somehow escaped.

From New York, it was on to Boston, where on the night of his arrival he went to sleep on a park bench. Then a policeman tapped him awake. Knowing that this officer had the power — and probably the desire — to put him behind bars, Johnny quickly fabricated a story about a dream he had just been having about his experiences in Japan. The policeman was enchanted by the tale — London said he listened appreciatively for two solid hours. And when he finished his tale, the officer gave him a quarter — which Johnny promptly spent for a steak and a cup of coffee in an all-night restaurant. This was probably the first time he was paid for one of his fictions!

Soon he met other tramps who told him where to find things in Boston, and he spent several days visiting the historical sites of the city and region — including Bunker Hill and the home of Paul Revere. He might well have wondered how the dream of the patriots had gone so wrong. He had seen it all firsthand: things were not fair across the land. There were masses of people who did not share in the American Dream. People may have been created equal, but they did not live as equals.

In a 1907 essay, "Hoboes That Pass in the Night," Jack London wrote about an odd experience he had in his three-thousand-mile journey home. In the Montreal train yard he came across the name "Skysail Jack" carved in plain view; along with the name was the information that this particular hobo had left the city only one day earlier. At this time, Johnny's nickname was "Sailor Jack," so he was naturally curious to find this hobo whose "monica" so closely resembled his own. Eight days later, three-hundred miles west of Ottawa, Johnny again came across the name, this time carved into a water tower. Johnny figured he was now two days behind, and his pride demanded that he catch this hobo.

As the days passed, other hoboes along the way told Johnny that Skysail Jack was interested in this Sailor Jack who was chasing him; he had asked a lot of questions. But he was determined to reach the West Coast first. At several points they changed the lead. Johnny would be a day or so ahead; then Skysail Jack would pass him once again. Near Vancouver, British Columbia, Johnny was trailing again, and when he finally arrived at the Pacific Ocean, he learned that Skysail Jack had beat him by about a day and had already shipped out, for an unknown destination. Johnny was disappointed. He had lost the cross-country race, and he had failed to meet this "tramp-royal" whose skills he admired so much. After a brief wait, Johnny landed a job as a coal-shoveler aboard the San Francisco-bound ship *Umatilla*.

He returned to Oakland a changed young man. He was nearing his nineteenth birthday, and he had seen enough of life in the factories, of life on the road and on the streets. In Baltimore, he had been inspired by the speech-makers in the park. They had awakened in him a desire to make his own voice heard — in writing and otherwise. They had also shown him that he was not ready for such a life. He needed a better education. There were books he needed to read — hundreds — no, *thousands* of them. And he could not wait to begin.

In his essay "What Life Means to Me" Jack London spelled out what he felt at this time in his life. "I had been born in the working class," he wrote, "and I was now, at the age of eighteen, beneath the point at which I had started. I was down in the cellar of society. . . . I was in the pit, the abyss, the human cesspool, the shambles and the charnel house* of our civilization." He went on: "The things I saw there gave me a terrible scare." He decided that it was his brain — his mind — that would save him. He knew that he was intelligent; he knew that he learned quickly. He also knew that a life of rough, physical labor would eventually weaken and destroy him, just as it had so many people he had seen at sea, in the cannery, in the jute mill.

Near the end of one of his stories, "The Apostate," he describes such a person, a boy whose name is also Johnny: "He did not walk like a man. He did not look like a man. He was a travesty of the human. It was a twisted and stunted and nameless piece of life that shambled like a sickly ape, arms loose-hanging, stoop-shouldered, narrow-chested, grotesque and terrible." He did not want to end up like this, twisted and broken. "So I was resolved to sell no more muscle," he declared, "and to become a vendor of brains." At the age of nineteen he returned to high school and enrolled as a ninth grader. There, he wrote, he began the "frantic pursuit of knowledge."

*A place where dead bodies were stored before burial.

FOUR

1894–1896: Back to School, Back to Work

I returned to California and opened the books.

— Jack London, "What Life Means to Me"

When Johnny arrived back in Oakland in December 1894, he discovered that his parents had moved once again. But they were glad to see him safe and healthy and were excited to hear about his many adventures on the road.

His father's health was not good and he was no longer capable of supporting the family. Flora still needed to give piano lessons and to conduct séances. Johnny would once again be expected to contribute, too.

So it was with some reluctance that Flora and John listened to their son's plan to return to school. But he promised them he would find work, any kind of work, if they would just agree to let him go. They did agree — and he was as good as his word. To help with family expenses during his high school period, he mowed lawns, beat carpets, and worked on the waterfront as a stevedore, loading and unloading ships. He took other odd jobs he could find as well.

With his stepsister Eliza's help he got a job at the school. At night he swept the rooms he studied in by

day. Years later, when his own daughter Joan entered
the same high school, he wrote to her:

> Please remember that I have swept every
> room in that old High School from garret
> [attic] to basement. Also, that I have
> hoisted the American flag every high
> school day for two terms on top of said
> old High School Building. Also, just for
> the fun of it, take a walk around the en-
> tire block occupied by the High School
> Building and look up at all the windows
> from the ground floor to the top floor
> and just get the idea into your head
> that every one of those windows I have
> washed in the past. I washed them inside
> and outside.

It was at the beginning of the second semester, in
January 1895, when Johnny London enrolled in Oakland High School. To help celebrate the beginning of
his new life, Eliza presented him with a bicycle. He
would need it: Oakland High School was a couple of
miles away. His mother, now accustomed to the idea,
helped him arrange one of the rooms in the house as
his bedroom-study. A big bed was against one wall; next
to it was a nightstand with a reading lamp and room for
a few books and notepads. On the opposite wall, below
a window, was a large table for his books and writing
materials. In one corner were a dresser and mirror.
When he went to bed, he would pull over near him another chair to hold a bowl of fruit. This was a habit for

Oakland High School, which Jack attended for one year

the rest of his life. He always kept snacks near his bed so he wouldn't fall asleep as he worked late into the night.

On the chair by his bed he also kept some cigarettes and matches, another lifelong habit. While at sea and on the road he had begun smoking; he would never really stop. His stepsister had known, of course, about his smoking, but she was surprised to discover that he now also liked to chew tobacco. Eliza would not stand for it. "And no brother of mine is going to take any chewing tobacco into high school in my town," she declared.

Johnny was embarrassed. He told Eliza that he

chewed in part to keep his teeth from hurting. He opened his mouth and showed Eliza quite a mess. While he was tramping, some "dentists" in Kelly's Army had pulled a number of his upper front teeth when he had complained of toothaches. Many others looked neglected — even diseased. She offered him a deal: if he would give up chewing tobacco, she would pay for new false upper teeth and for drilling and filling the others. He promptly agreed. When the teeth had been made for him, he proudly displayed them to his sister — and announced that he had just bought a toothbrush, the first he had ever owned. Now he was ready for high school.

Johnny London created quite a stir among his much younger classmates, and he must have felt very awkward sitting in classrooms with students whose lives and experiences had been so different from his. Compared to him, they were children. He was nineteen years old, and given his activities of the past few years, was anything but a typical high school freshman.

One of his classmates, Georgia Loring, recalled very clearly what it was like to be in class with Johnny London in Oakland High School. She noticed him on the first day of class — "a strange boy," she called him, "a very strange boy." She even recalled his clothing that day: "He wore a dark blue suit, much worn, mussed, wrinkled and ill-fitting and a woolen shirt without a tie. His face was ruddy and sunburned, and his tawny, disheveled hair looked as though he constantly ran his fingers through it. His general appearance was really unbelievably shabby, careless and uncleanly; unlike anything I had ever seen in a school room."

Johnny was very busy in high school. He devoted most of his time to studying and working, but he also joined some of the academic clubs the school sponsored — including the Henry Clay Debating Society. There he practiced and improved the skills he had admired in the men who had spoken so passionately about politics back in the park in Baltimore.

The school also had a club that published a literary journal called the *Aegis*. The name (pronounced *EE-jus*) means *shield*, and it can also mean *protection*. In this magazine Johnny published ten pieces of writing. Beneath the title of his first story in the Oakland High School *Aegis* was the name "John London"; but the rest bore the name "Jack London," the name he used for his writing forever afterward.

He was a fast worker. "Bonin Islands — An Incident of the Sealing Fleet of '93," the first of his efforts, appeared in the issue of January 18, 1895, only a couple of weeks after he had begun to attend high school. On February 15 another one was published — this one a story about road-kids called "'Frisco Kid's Story." Following were more stories about sailing and tramping; there was an essay about education; there was even a murder mystery, "Who Believes in Ghosts?"

"One More Unfortunate" — the last story Jack published in the *Aegis* — is a touching tale about an unnamed country boy who has been inspired by something he has read — Ouida's *Signa*, Jack's own boyhood favorite. The boy saves his money to travel to the big city to study the violin. There, he at first finds some success. But gradually, inevitably, his little store of money runs out, so he performs before loud, rude crowds in saloons and music halls. And then one night, playing to one of the raucous crowds, he realizes his life has flown past. His dreams are unfulfilled, his talent now diminished. Devastated, he leaves the music hall and staggers down to the waterfront where he stares at the sea and — London leads us to believe — takes his own life. "One More Unfortunate" is, of course, not just the story of an old violinist who never realizes his dreams; it is the story that reveals the fears of Jack London. He did not want to turn out like this old man. He would be true to his talent.

While he was attending high school, Jack continued his voracious reading. He claimed to have more than a half-dozen cards from the Oakland Public Library, for he was allowed to take out only a few books on one card, and a few books were not nearly enough for his active, eager mind. He was impatient to read everything as fast as he could.

He also joined a local socialist club where he studied and discussed politics, economics, and philosophy. "The whole tramping experience," he wrote later, "made me become a socialist."

One of his articles for the *Aegis* helps explain what he meant by *socialist*. "Pessimism, Optimism, and Patriotism" appeared in March of 1895 when he had just turned nineteen. In this essay he reveals that he believes that American society is divided into groups — or classes — based on money and power. At the bottom are what he called "the masses" — the uneducated and undereducated working people and unemployed. Having grown up among them, he knew this sort of people well. He had associated with them at sea, on the road, in prison, and in saloons all across the land. Above these people were the "prosperous middle and autocratic higher classes" — people with more money and power. And he also identified another, educated class — "our university and collegiate bred men." In his essay in the *Aegis*, London cried out for a cause he believed in very deeply — the education of everyone. All people, he believed, should be in the educated class, not just the rich and the privileged.

During his high school days, Jack also wrote some letters to the local newspapers on a variety of political topics. For example, on Christmas Day in 1895, his letter "What Socialism Is" appeared in the *San Francisco Examiner*. In it, he wrote: "Any man is a socialist who strives for a better form of Government than the one he is living under. Socialism means a reconstruction of society with a more just [fair] application of labor and distribution of the returns thereof. It cries out, 'Every one according to his deeds!' . . . Its moral foundation, 'All men are created equal,' and its ultimate aim is pure democracy."

He must have been dismayed when he read the article, though, for his name was misprinted as *Jack Loudon*. And the little article right next to his letter had the headline: JACK LOUDON, SOCIALIST. A small cartoon showed three views of Jack, dressed in a formal suit and lecturing.

In Jack's letters to the newspapers in 1895 and 1896, he wrote about how poor people ought to be helped by other people who could afford it and how wealth should be shared by many, not hoarded by a few. He believed that communities should share their work and their profits, not compete with one another. He once used the example of a ten-thousand-acre wheat ranch. Operating this ranch as one ranch, he thought, would be far more efficient than dividing it up into a hundred smaller ranches and having ranchers compete for sales of the wheat. The latter created, he believed, a system of winners and losers — a bad system, he thought.

He wrote about how working conditions ought to be more humane — workers should have shorter hours, longer vacations, better salaries, better benefits. He did not believe children should be laboring in factories. He thought that people should be able to retire, to receive a pension, and not have to work until they died.

One of Jack's friends during this time was Edward "Ted" Applegarth. Ted's father, a mining engineer from

Drawing of Jack from the San Francisco Chronicle, *16 February 1896*

England, had only recently moved his family to Oakland. Ted and Jack were fellow members of the Henry Clay Debating Society at the high school.

Ted must have been amazed to learn of Jack's background. The Applegarths were cultured and educated, so different from Jack. At the beginning of their friendship, Jack probably felt very awkward around Ted, too; he had never known anyone his own age like this young man who spoke with the strange accent and seemed so gentle — and who seemed surprised, maybe even shocked, when Jack swore, which was often.

One day, Ted invited Jack home to meet the rest of his family, including his sister, Mabel, who was more than two years older. Jack was absolutely dazzled by her. She seemed to him like one of the heroines in the adventure novels he loved. She was beautiful and intelligent. She could recite poetry and play the piano. And she was so *proper* — not at all like the women he had known in the factories and the saloons.

Jack later wrote a novel, *Martin Eden*, about a character very much like himself. Near the beginning of the story is a scene where a rough young sailor (Martin Eden) first meets a friend's sister named Ruth Morse. She is a young woman in many ways like Mabel. At the moment of their meeting Martin is looking at some books: "And then he turned and saw the girl. . . . She was a pale, ethereal [delicate] creature, with wide, spiritual blue eyes and a wealth of golden hair. . . . He likened her to a pale gold flower upon a slender stem. No, she was a spirit, a divinity, a goddess. . . ."

Jack began going regularly to the Applegarths', playing chess with Ted, simply enjoying being around Mabel, eating enormous helpings of whatever food Mrs. Applegarth set before him, and occasionally embarrassing himself by blurting out a swearword when Ted beat him in chess.

When the Oakland High School spring semester ended in 1895, Ted invited Jack to join the Applegarths for a vacation in Yosemite Park. When Jack visited, it was a California state park, somewhat smaller than its current size. The Applegarths had decided to go there because Mabel was ill, and the dry mountain climate would be an improvement over the damp waterfront air back in Oakland. Jack claimed later that he rode by horseback the ninety-five miles from the train depot at Fresno to Yosemite, "clad in almost tropical nudity, with a ball room fan and a silk parasol."

Jack's summer idyll did not last long. Soon it was back to Oakland, back to work, back to school. Throughout that fall, his stories and articles continued to appear in the *Aegis*. He also continued to participate actively in the debating society, to develop his chess-playing skills, to read everything he could, and to send fiery letters to the editors of the local newspapers.

At the end of the summer he met a new librarian at the Oakland Public Library. Frederick Irons Bamford was a thoughtful, scholarly man who would have an enormous influence on him. Bamford was more than twenty years older than the passionate young "Boy Socialist of Oakland." But he, too, was very interested in

Jack, the Applegarths, and friends in Yosemite; Jack stands just left of center

socialism, and because he had done even more reading than Jack — and had gone to college — he was able to give Jack's reading more direction and focus. Bamford was inspired by Jack's fierce determination and bright ideas. They often discussed books at the library — or stole away for lunch. They would remain friends and correspondents for the rest of Jack's life.

In January 1896 Jack reached his twentieth birthday and seemed well on his way to becoming the "brain
merchant" he hoped to be. But things appeared to be
moving so slowly. There was much about high school
he did not like. The students seemed young and im-
mature. And in many ways, he thought his teachers
were inadequate. They were boring. They had not traveled as widely as he had; some had not even read as
much as he had. They were not tolerant of his socialist
ideas — his zealousness made them uncomfortable.
Eager to get on with his life, Jack decided to drop out
of Oakland High School. "I grew impatient," he explained later.

In the 1890s it was possible to be admitted to a
university without a high school diploma if the appli-
cant passed an entrance examination. Very close to
Oakland — only about ten miles north — is the town
of Berkeley, home of a branch of the University of
California. Jack knew that he could not afford to attend a university any farther away from home — be-
sides, his parents needed the little income he brought
in. So he decided to skip the remaining three years of
high school and take Berkeley's entrance examinations
in August.

In Alameda, California, very near his home, there
was what he called a "cramming joint" — a place that
specialized in preparing young people for the entrance
tests. It was called Anderson's University Academy.
Jack borrowed the academy's fee from his stepsister

Eliza, rode his bike across the bridge to Alameda, and enrolled, attempting to compress the two-year curriculum of the school into the four months remaining before the tests.

For five weeks he studied like a man possessed, desperately trying to force into his brain the four subjects the test would measure: mathematics, history, physics, and English. Then, to his shock, the director of the academy called him in and told him he would have to leave. Jack's performance was fine. But the director was worried that the University of California would question the academy's credentials if it permitted a student to do what Jack was doing in so short a time.

Jack's daughter Joan believed there was another reason: she felt Mr. Anderson was embarrassed by the superior performance of the poor boy from Oakland's East End. The wealthy students resented this rough, uncultured youth, and Mr. Anderson was afraid of losing their business. He returned the fee, and Jack, stunned and hurt, slowly rode his bike back across the bridge from Alameda to Oakland.

But Jack was not one to sulk about a failure. Instead, he did some quick mental calculations. There were twelve weeks remaining before the test; there were twenty-four hours in each day. He would make use of as many of those hours as he could and simply teach himself. He would withdraw from the library all the high school textbooks he would need. He would ask some friends to help him with some of the subjects. And he would march into those entrance examinations in August and pass them, academy or no academy. Jack figured he could teach himself the history and English he would need, but he recruited Fred Jacobs, a high school student who worked at the public library, to help him with physics, and for math he got help from Bessie Maddern, a young woman his friend Ted Applegarth had introduced him to. She was six months younger than Jack, but she taught mathematics privately — and she, too, was studying for the exams.

At home, he transformed his little room into an office and began to study. Later, he would write about this extraordinary intellectual effort: "Nineteen hours a day I studied. For three months I kept this pace, only breaking it on several occasions. My body grew weary,

Jack, with Bessie Maddern (left) and Mabel Applegarth, around 1900

my mind grew weary, but I stayed with it. My eyes grew weary and began to twitch, but they did not break down."

On August 10, 1896, Jack rode his bike to the Mechanics' Building on the Berkeley campus. The tests were distributed. He was so exhausted from his efforts to prepare that he did not even notice at the time that the questions were harder than the ones on the practice tests he had used. The university officials felt that too many students were qualifying for entrance — they didn't have room for them all — and so, without any warning, they simply made the tests more difficult.

By the time Jack finished, he was absolutely drained. "I didn't want to see a book," he wrote later. "I didn't want to think nor to lay eyes on anybody who was liable to think." He did what he frequently did when his mind was numb from study, his body weary from work: he went down to the waterfront. He packed some food and blankets, borrowed a small boat, and sailed out onto the San Francisco Bay he knew so well. It was early in the morning; the fog made the water appear to be smoking. He took a familiar route: across San Pablo Bay to the Carquinez Straits and the town of Benicia. There, responding to an urge he had nearly forgotten, he decided to go ashore to look for old friends . . . and for a drink. "For the first time in my life," he wrote, "I consciously, deliberately desired to get drunk."

It didn't take long. Almost immediately he found Charley Le Grant, his partner on the Fish Patrol. Billy

Murphy and Joe Lloyd, other friends from those days, joined the party, and they all headed for Jorgensen's Saloon. Soon other old friends gathered for the reunion. Beer and whiskey flowed freely.

Later that night, Charley helped the dazed and dizzy Jack into his boat and off he sailed into the waves that were tossing fiercely in a high wind. Somehow he managed to stay afloat until he entered the San Joaquin River and safely put ashore at Antioch, California, where he once again ran into some old friends who gave him food and shelter for the night. He was lucky to be alive.

For a week Jack continued his cruise along the river, but — except for one slipup — he managed to avoid further drinking. He returned to Oakland to learn the results of his entrance tests. He had passed. Jack London, the grammar school graduate who had completed only a year of high school, had been accepted at the great University of California at Berkeley.

Jack entered the university in the fall of 1896 — the Class of 1900. To pay his fees, it is probable that he borrowed — once again — from his stepsister Eliza. He signed up for English 1 (Types of English Prose Style), English 11 (General History of English Literature), History 1 (History of Europe During the Middle Ages), History 111 (History from the Reformation to the French Revolution), Military Science and Tactics, and Physical Culture. His grades that term were fairly good — some B's, an A. A couple of courses did not list a grade, only "no report." This may mean that he did not complete all the work, or perhaps he dropped out.

A classmate from Oakland High, James Hopper, remembered seeing Jack at Berkeley. He recalled that Jack had a reputation among the other young men on campus as "one who had done man things and wild things and romantic things." He also remembered how Jack looked and dressed in those days: "He had a curly mop of hair . . . and his eyes were like a sunlit sea. His clothes were flappy and careless; . . . he was a strange combination of a Scandinavian sailor and Greek god, made altogether boyish and lovable by the lack of two front teeth. . . ."

But Jack's time in college was a struggle. He was studying hard; he had no money; he had few opportunities to be with Mabel Applegarth and his other friends. "Do you know what I suffered during that High School and University period?" he later wrote to Mabel. "The imps of hell would have wept had they been with me. Does any one know? Can any one know?"

One of Jack's less successful moments at the university came in the gymnasium, where he liked to go to work out and box. Boxing was the most popular sport in America during Jack's lifetime, and it was common at the end of the nineteenth century for young men to join athletic clubs so they could learn to box and compete against other clubs.

Jack, of course, had learned most of his fighting skills in the more practical schools on the streets and waterfront, aboard ships, in prison, and in train yards. He was not a large man — about five feet eight inches tall — but he was sturdy and strong from all his physical labor, and he was a fearless fighter. Until the very end of his life he would occasionally get into scraps with people in saloons, coming home late at night with a bloody nose and a tale to tell. Later, he covered boxing matches for newspapers and wrote two boxing novels — *The Game* (1905) and *The Abysmal Brute* (1913). Jack and his wife Charmian liked to spar for exercise.

At Berkeley, Jack convinced another freshman to put on the gloves with him and then quickly knocked the young man out by using the "wild-cat" technique he had found effective at sea and in his street fights: he swung wildly and enthusiastically — like a windmill. When one of his punches connected, his opponent slumped senseless to the floor. Nearby, an older student — a junior — was watching. He confronted Jack, reproaching him for taking advantage of a smaller, less experienced man. Angry, Jack swung without warning, but the junior was an athlete and easily dodged the blow. Another battle began.

Again, Jack employed his windmill style, but the junior was a practiced boxer and effortlessly dodged and blocked the violent flurry of blows. When Jack was just about exhausted, the junior struck. Jack found himself in an unfamiliar position: on the floor, dazed, humiliated in front of the small crowd of spectators. He struggled to his feet and ran from the gymnasium.

While Jack was attending university, his family moved once again, this time only a few blocks away to a larger two-story house surrounded by a white picket fence. Flora was still giving piano lessons and conducting séances, but John London was growing weaker and could not bring to the family a dependable income. Flora had to turn to her son, once again, for financial support. Jack would have to withdraw from the university. On February 4, 1897, he left Berkeley. He would never again return to school.

"I was not very disappointed," Jack wrote later. The financial pressures on his family were real, he knew, and he was not very excited about the classes he was taking or about the professors who were teaching him. "The university was not giving me all that I wanted in the time I could spare for it," he said. Again, he felt his education was moving too slowly. He was impatient. He wanted to get on with it. He was also becoming much more confident in himself; he had enormous faith in books and in his ability to learn from them. He frequently referred to his books as his "tools," and he used them for the remainder of his life as a substitute for teachers.

On his way to the Oakland Public Library — always a favorite spot — Jack would pass through City Hall Park where he often heard people making public speeches, just as he had back in Baltimore during his tramping days. Occasionally, he would stop and listen, maybe even argue socialist ideas with the speaker. One day he began making speeches of his own. Soon he was drawing crowds and receiving notice in newspapers on both sides of the Bay.

The *San Francisco Chronicle* reported in February 1896 — before Jack had even entered Berkeley — that there were many speakers in City Hall Park, but Jack "always gets the biggest crowds and the most respectful attention. . . . The young man is a pleasant speaker, more earnest than eloquent. . . ."

He had also been attending regular meetings of the Socialist Labor Party in Oakland and had participated in other political activities as well. At one of these meetings the group discussed a city ordinance in Oakland that the socialists found offensive — Ordinance No. 1676, which prohibited people from speaking in the city without first receiving permission from the mayor. The socialists and other speakers in the park thought this was unconstitutional. After all, didn't the Constitution guarantee free speech for all? And freedom of assembly? The socialists wanted one of their group to provoke an arrest to test the law, then to see how a judge and jury would respond. Jack was quick to volunteer.

On February 10, 1897, only about a week after he left the university, Jack stood up in the park and began speaking. A crowd gathered, and soon enough the police arrived. When Jack refused to stop speaking, they arrested him and took him off to jail — not an unfamiliar place for the "Boy Socialist." At his trial on February 18, Jack served as his own lawyer and presented a case convincing enough to most of the jurors: all but one voted "not guilty," and the judge dismissed the charges. Jack found himself, for the briefest of moments, an even greater celebrity in the Bay Area, especially among his socialist companions.

After he left the university, he was not able to find work immediately. He convinced his mother to give him just a little more time; surely he could sell some of his writing. "Heavens, how I wrote!" he said. He sat in his room and wrote as much as fifteen hours a day, seven days a week.

He wrote a little bit of everything during this period — short stories, poems, jokes, essays, and articles about science and sociology. He claimed even to have written a blank-verse tragedy in the style of Shakespeare. He mailed off everything to magazines in New York, Boston, and Philadelphia, the great publishing centers in the East.

He wrote everything in longhand, then at night borrowed a typewriter from his brother-in-law, James Shepard, who used it only during the days. Early typewriters had no shift key, so all letters were capitals. London wrote later that this particular machine seemed possessed by "an evil spirit." He could not seem to make it behave the way he wanted it to. "The keys of that machine had to be hit so hard that to one outside the house it sounded like distant thunder or someone breaking up the furniture," he complained. "I had to hit the keys so hard that I strained my first fingers to the elbows, while the ends of my fingers were blisters burst and blistered again. Had it been my machine I'd have operated it with a carpenter's hammer."

For stamps and paper and envelopes he borrowed money, pawned his possessions, and begged his parents to be patient. He would succeed. He just knew it. This wild, passionate attempt to succeed as a writer was similar in many ways to his windmill style of boxing. He figured if he swung at every magazine editor in the East, maybe he would get lucky and connect.

But the editors dodged his manuscripts as easily as that junior had slipped his frantic punches back in the Berkeley gymnasium. They rejected every single item he sent to them. "My manuscripts," Jack wrote later, "made amazing round-trip records between the Pacific and the Atlantic."

Relations with his family were souring. There was now another member of the household to feed — Johnny Miller, the two-year-old son of John London's daughter Ida. Her husband, Frank, had abandoned her in 1892, and she was paying Flora to watch the little boy while she worked. Jack was not contributing much to the family's income, but he was eating, using electricity, wearing clothes. The Londons could not afford to support him like this, especially since John's health was so unpredictable.

It was during this time that Jack learned something that shocked him horribly. Someone — perhaps one of his relatives who was jealous of his education and growing fame — told him that John London was not really his father. He hurried across the bay to the newspaper offices in San Francisco and read the brief notice of his birth. He probably also found the item about Flora's attempted suicide when William Chaney told her to abort the baby that would become Jack. He discovered that Chaney was in Chicago — and had been there while he had visited the ruins of the World's Fair in 1894! In the spring of 1897, he wrote Chaney two different letters, inquiring if the old astrologer were in fact his father.

Chaney responded twice, on June 4 and June 14. In both letters he steadfastly denied being Jack's father. In fact, he denied even being married to Flora. He also claimed that he could not have been a father because he was "impotent at that time, the result of hardship, privation [lack of necessities] & too much brain-work. Therefore I cannot be your father, nor am I sure who your father is." There is no record of any further correspondence or contact between Jack London and W. H. Chaney.

Most people who have studied Jack's family and background believe that Chaney was Jack's father. There is no real proof that Flora had relations with anyone else — and she certainly believed Chaney was the man. Jack himself never mentioned Chaney in any of his published writing. And in his letters, he always referred to John London as his father, which, in every meaningful way, he was.

With the help of Herbert Shepard (the stepson of Jack's stepsister Eliza), Jack soon found a job in the laundry at the Belmont Academy where Herbert worked. The academy was a military school for boys in the countryside south of San Francisco. "We worked like tigers," London wrote, especially when the summer months arrived and the young men began wearing their "white-duck" trousers — pants made from a heavy cotton fabric. The two did not discover until later that they had replaced four men.

For all this effort, Jack was receiving thirty dollars a month plus room and board. He had Sundays off. He had hoped that he could continue his reading and other studies while he was at the academy and had brought with him a supply of books and writing materials. But he quickly found that he was simply too exhausted by the end of each day and by the end of the week to do anything but fall into bed.

Jack and Herbert did devise one prankish form of entertainment for themselves. Because they also did the laundry for the teachers at the academy — and their wives — they decided to add extra starch to the women's underthings, stiffening them so much that they must have felt like cardboard. In the 1890s the women would have been far too modest to complain about the condition of their underwear, so Jack and Herbert had the private pleasure of knowing that they were making others feel at least a portion of the discomfort they were feeling.

Discouraged and exhausted, Jack soon left the Belmont Academy laundry, once again determined to avoid jobs that made him into a "work beast" and to try to make his way in the world with his intelligence instead of his physical strength. Back in Oakland, Jack looked around for some sort of temporary job. He needed a salary big enough to contribute to the needs of the family — with a little left over for later when he would once again try writing. He had not given up this dream. "I was not disappointed," he wrote later. "My career was retarded, that was all. Perhaps I did need further preparation. I had learned enough from the books to realize that I had touched only the hem of knowledge's garment. . . . My waking hours, and most of the hours I should have used for sleep, were spent with the books."

And then, on July 15, 1897, a ship from Alaska named *Excelsior* dropped anchor in San Francisco. It was loaded with gold and miners who reported a fabulous gold strike, two thousand miles north, in the Klondike River region of the Canadian Yukon. Millions of dollars in gold were there for the taking. The story was front-page news around the world — and became all the more believable when another ship, the *Portland*, arrived two days later in Seattle, Washington, also stuffed with Klondike gold and grinning miners.

A tremendous stampede northward followed almost immediately. Tens of thousands of people left their homes and jobs and charged into the Northland in a fantastic race for the Klondike gold. And among those leading that charge was young Jack London.

THE SEATTLE POST-INTELLIGENCER.

VOL. XXXII. No. 62.   SEATTLE, WASHINGTON, SATURDAY, JULY 17, 1897.   EIGHT-PAGE EDITION.

LATEST NEWS FROM THE KLONDIKE.
9 O'CLOCK EDITION.

GOLD! GOLD! GOLD! GOLD!

Sixty-Eight Rich Men on the Steamer Portland.

STACKS OF YELLOW METAL!

Some Have $5,000, Many Have More, and a Few Bring Out $100,000 Each.

THE STEAMER CARRIES $700,000.

Special Tug Chartered by the Post-Intelligencer to Get the News.

THE LAND OF GOLD.

News of the Klondike gold strike reaches Seattle, starting the stampede north

FIVE

1897–1898: Gold! Gold! Gold!

Yes, I had let career go hang, and was
on the adventure-path again in quest
of fortune.
— Jack London, *John Barleycorn*

The Klondike gold rush was one of the most astonishing events in American history. Perhaps as many as one hundred thousand people actually left home to join the river of humanity flowing northward into one of the most primitive places on earth. A place where there were no roads, no railroads, no stores, no towns, neither telephone nor telegraph. A place populated only by a few scattered tribes of American Indians. A place where grizzly bears and wolves roamed. A place where temperatures in the winter plummeted to 40, 50, 60, even 70 degrees below zero. To get there, most gold seekers had to travel thousands of miles, hike over the Coast Mountains of Alaska, navigate hundreds of miles of the mighty Yukon River — and carry everything they would need to survive on their backs and in their boats. None of this stopped the waves of men, women, and even children who surged into the Yukon. If a fortune lay at the other end, why not give it a try? After all, weren't nuggets of gold as big as eggs just lying around for the taking?

Gold seekers leave San Francisco for the North

The main route to the North was traveled by tens of thousands. From San Francisco or Seattle the gold rushers went by steamship to the southeastern coast of Alaska, about one hundred miles north of Juneau at the foot of the Coast Mountains. There, two small towns quickly became cities of thousands. The first was Skagway; the other, about nine miles up the coast, was Dyea (pronounced *die-EE*). From either of these two towns, the gold seekers next had to cross the rugged mountains that rise steeply right from the ocean. At Skagway and Dyea are two of the only trails through those mountains. All other passes are clogged with glaciers.

Those who landed at Dyea had to cross the Chilkoot Pass; from Skagway, it was the White Pass. Both were extremely difficult and dangerous. An avalanche on the Chilkoot killed more than sixty people in the spring of 1898, and the White Pass trail was so rough and rocky and steep that no pack animal made it across the first year. It earned the name "Dead Horse Trail" because the carcasses of thousands of animals lay along the way. At times miners had to walk on top of their fallen bodies.

At the top of the passes, about fifteen miles from the ocean, is the border of Alaska and British Columbia. Waiting there were members of the North-west Mounted Police — the Canadian Mounties — who would not let people continue if they did not have with them a year's supply of food. Starvation was certain

Dyea, Alaska, in 1897

without it. This meant, for the average person, about a ton of goods. Because no person can carry two thousand pounds, it was necessary for each gold prospector to make repeated trips up and down the Chilkoot and White Pass trails in order to carry everything.

But once the gold rushers reached the summit of the mountains with their ton of goods, and once they convinced the North-west Mounted Police that they were sufficiently equipped to go on, their journey had only just begun. Before them lay another fifteen miles or so of extremely rugged trail to one of two lakes, Lindeman or Bennett, which were connected by deadly one-mile rapids. Once again, they would have to make repeated trips back and forth to the passes to transport their supplies to the lake shore. There, the prospectors built boats and rafts large enough for themselves and all their supplies. For once they crossed the lakes, they could enter the Yukon River and float the remaining five hundred miles or so to Dawson City.

It was Jack's stepsister Eliza who once again helped him do something he could not otherwise have afforded. Her husband, James Shepard, was in his mid-fifties when the rush began, but the gold bug had bitten him deeply, and he wanted to join the great stampede. He knew he would need help, and so he offered Jack a proposition: he would pay all Jack's expenses if the younger man would travel with him and give him a hand when he needed it. Shepard did not have to make the offer twice. The next day Eliza took Jack across the Bay for a shopping spree in San Francisco. Her money did not last long: they bought heavy coats, fur caps, mittens, boots, and other warm clothing so necessary in the North.

Jack wrote a quick letter to Mabel Applegarth, the woman he loved, telling her what he was about to do. She did not answer but her mother did, surely at the urging of a very worried Mabel. "Oh, dear John," she pleaded, "do be persuaded to give up the idea for we feel certain that you are going to meet your death and we shall never see you again. . . . Your father and mother must be nearly crazed over it. Now, even at the eleventh hour, dear John, do change your mind and stay."

Not a chance.

On July 25, 1897, only ten days after news of the gold strike had reached San Francisco, Jack and his brother-in-law stepped aboard the steamship *Umatilla* — the same ship, coincidentally, on which Jack had sailed home at the end of his tramping trip. Aboard the *Umatilla*, Jack and James Shepard met and joined forces with several other men — Merritt Sloper, Jim Goodman, and Fred Thompson. Historians are grateful for Fred Thompson's presence on this trip because he kept a diary. They would travel together the rest of the way and help one another. The *Umatilla* took the men as far as Port Townsend, Washington, about thirty miles northwest of Seattle, where they transferred to the *City of Topeka*, bound for Juneau, Alaska. In a letter, Jack said that he bought a Klondike sled — the very type that the dogs would pull in Jack's Northland stories.

On August 2 the *City of Topeka* arrived in Juneau, where Jack and his party hired some Chilkat Indians to transport them by canoe the remaining one hundred miles to Dyea. While he was in Dyea, Jack wrote a letter to Mabel. He was, he said, lying in the grass at the time. He compared the scenery to the landscape he and Mabel had seen in the Yosemite Valley, with "glaciers and waterfalls on every side." He described an avalanche: "The rumble and roar extended for fully a minute." He told her that the Chilkat canoes had been loaded with men, women, children, and even dogs. He then told her that he expected to be carrying one-hundred-pound packs to the summit of the Chilkoot Pass; his strategy was to carry each load about a mile, add it to his pile, then return for the next one.

As they began up the trail, Shepard realized very soon that he could not tolerate the heat, the carrying, and the rugged, rocky conditions. He decided to return to California — though he left Jack with enough money and supplies to finish the journey. A day later another man, named Tarwater, joined their party. He would appear in one of Jack London's stories, "Like Argus of the Ancient Times," as a character named John "Old Man" Tarwater.

The passage to the summit was extremely difficult for all of them. They quickly developed blisters on their feet and backs. It was hot and muggy much of the way, for on the Alaska side of the mountains the trail passes through a rain forest. It rained much of the time, forcing the men to cope with an increasingly slippery trail

The Chilkoot Pass, winter of 1897–1898

and with muddy clothing. Yet, as they neared the top of the pass they found snow.

While Jack was scaling the Chilkoot, he noticed a pair of feet sticking up out of the snow. He took off his own pack and dug around near the feet. He found the man attached to them — still alive. The unfortunate hiker had been sitting on a log, and his overweight pack

had caused him to topple over backward into a snow-
drift. He could neither cry out nor stand up. If Jack had
not happened by, he would have suffocated.

By the end of August, Jack and his partners had
packed most of their supplies to the top of the pass.
The rain had been constant, and they had to hike two
miles from their camp to find any firewood. Other stam-
peders had cut every nearby tree.

Slowly, painfully, they moved their outfit the remaining fifteen miles to the shores of Lake Lindeman,
where they made camp on September 8, 1897. Jack set
out with Merritt Sloper to find a stand of trees so they
could cut the lumber to make their boats. In a little
over a week, they completed the first one, and by mid-
September they were ready to load their two new vessels, now named *Belle of the Yukon* and *Yukon Belle.*
Each was about twenty-seven feet long and designed to
carry several tons.

While Jack labored long hours in the lingering
Northland twilight, it would have pleased him to know
that back in Boston, the September issue of a magazine
called *The Owl* contained his short story "Two Gold
Bricks." It was a silly story about spiritualists and a con-
game, but it was the first time his work had appeared in
a national magazine. But Jack apparently did not ever
learn of its publication, and he never received any payment for it.

To get to Lake Bennett and the headwaters of the
Yukon River, they first had to portage their boats and
supplies around the rapids that connect lakes Linde-

The Miles Canyon Rapids on the Yukon River

man and Bennett. It would have been quicker to run the rapids, but they were afraid of losing everything in the wild water. By September 22, they were on Lake Bennett and in a desperate race to beat "freeze-up"; if the river closed before they reached Dawson City, they knew they would have to go ashore and camp for the rest of the winter and not reach the goldfields until spring.

When they arrived at Miles Canyon on September 25, they pulled ashore and walked downriver for a look. The canyon rapids looked frightening and strange: a steep ridge of water formed in the very center of the river. It was difficult to talk over the roar of

the water slamming into the canyon walls, but they decided not to carry their supplies around. They had lost
too much time already, so they would shoot the rapids,
risking everything in a frantic ride between the granite
cliffs. They knew that as soon as they emerged from the
canyon — if they survived — they would enter the
even deadlier Whitehorse Rapids. But Jack was confident in his abilities with a boat. Years of training in the
San Francisco Bay and the Sacramento River had prepared him for these next terrifying moments. Later Jack
wrote:

> I caught a glimpse of the spectators
> fringing the brink of the cliffs above,
> and another glimpse of the rock walls
> dashing by like twin lightning express
> trains; then my whole energy was concen-
> trated in keeping to the Ridge. This was
> serrated with stiff waves, which the
> boat, dead with weight, could not mount,
> being forced to jab her nose through at
> every lunge. For all the peril, I caught
> myself smiling at the ridiculous capers
> cut by Sloper, perched in the very bow
> and working his paddle like mad. Just as
> he would let drive for a tremendous
> stroke, the stern would fall in a
> trough, jerking the bow clear up, and he
> would miss the water utterly. And at the
> next stroke, perhaps, the nose would
> dive clean under, almost sweeping him
> away – and he only weighed one hundred
> pounds. But never did he lose his pres-

ence of mind or grit. Once, he turned and cried some warning at the top of his lungs, but it was drowned in the pandemonium of sound. The next instant we fell off the Ridge. The water came inboard in all directions, and the boat, caught in a transverse current, threatened to twist broadside. This would mean destruction. I threw myself against the sweep [steering device] till I could hear it cracking, while Sloper snapped his paddle short off.*

And all this time we were flying down the gutter, less than two yards from the wall. Several times it seemed all up with us; but finally, mounting the Ridge almost sidewise, we took a header through a tremendous comber [wave] and shot into the whirlpool of the great circular court.

Ordering out the oars for steerageway, and keeping a close eye on the split currents, I caught one free breath before we flew into the second half of the canyon. Though we crossed the Ridge from left to right and back again, it was merely a repetition of the first half. A moment later the <u>Yukon Belle</u> rubbed softly against the bank. We had run the mile of canyon in two minutes by the watch.

*The powerful current broke off Sloper's paddle.

Jack and Sloper walked back the way they had come and helped a friend run his boat through — "a ticklish affair," Jack said, because the boat was smaller and more heavily loaded. But they rocketed through the canyon without incident.

And then they were ready for the Whitehorse Rapids.

Again, Jack and his partners decided not to portage their goods around; it would take four days, they estimated. And so, flush with the excitement of the successful Miles Canyon runs, they decided to shoot the rapids that roared and foamed whitely before them. They climbed back in the *Yukon Belle* and shoved off from the shore. They apparently had few problems — until they reached what was called "the Mane of the Horse," which Jack described as "a succession of foamy, mountainous waves."

```
When we struck the "Mane," the Yukon
Belle forgot her heavy load, taking a
series of leaps almost clear of the wa-
ter, alternating with as many burials in
the troughs. To this day I cannot see
how it happened, but I lost control. A
cross current caught our stern and we
began to swing broadside. Then we jumped
into the whirlpool, though I did not
guess it at the time. Sloper snapped a
second paddle and received another duck-
ing.
    It must be remembered that we were
traveling at racehorse speed, and that
```

things happened in a tithe [tenth] of the time taken to tell them. From every quarter the water came aboard, threatening to swamp us. The Yukon Belle headed directly for the jagged left bank, and though I was up against the steering sweep till it cracked, I could not turn her nose downstream. Onlookers from the shore tried to snapshot us, but failed to gauge our speed or get more than a wild view of angry waters and flying foam.

The bank was alarmingly close, but the boat still had the bit in her teeth. It was all happening so quickly, that I for the first time realized I was trying to buck the whirlpool. Like a flash I was bearing against the opposite side of the sweep. The boat answered, at the same time following the bent of the whirlpool, and headed upstream. But the shave was so close that Sloper leaped to the top of a rock. Then, on seeing we had missed by a couple of inches, he pluckily tumbled aboard, all in a heap, like a man boarding a comet.

Though tearing like mad through a whirlpool, we breathed freer. Completing the circle, we were thrown into the "Mane," which we shot a second time and safely landed in a friendly eddy below.

One of the most frequently published stories about Jack London is the tale that he was so successful at the Whitehorse Rapids that he lingered there for a few days and made three thousand dollars piloting other boats through for twenty-five dollars apiece. This story is not true. According to Fred Thompson's diary, Jack and Sloper went back to pilot only one other boat, for a Mr. and Mrs. Ret — the same people they had helped at Miles Canyon.

Each day the weather grew colder, and they encountered more and more slush in the river. The Yukon was freezing, and for days they floated through the thickening liquid — it must have felt as if they were trying to sail in frigid pancake batter.

On October 9, 1897, they arrived at the mouth of the Stewart River, about seventy miles short of Dawson City. There are several sizable islands here, and on one of them ("Upper Island") they found some abandoned cabins. Because they were worried about the freezing river, and because they were also concerned that there would be no accommodations for them in Dawson, they decided to move into the cabins and use them as their base for the winter.

For the first few days Jack and his partners settled in their cabins and did a little prospecting. Jim Goodman and Jack went up nearby Henderson Creek, looking for likely spots. They staked some claims, and Jack's name appears on Claim No. 54 on the left fork of the creek. Later this spot would figure in one of his most famous stories, "To Build a Fire." In the story, an unnamed traveler is out with his dog on a brutally cold day. "But the temperature did not matter. He was bound for the old claim on the left fork of Henderson Creek, where the boys were already." Later in the story, the man learns that such cold temperatures *do* matter.

Because the river had not yet closed, Jack and his partners decided to head down to Dawson to register their claims and to take a look at this new city that they had heard so much about. On Monday, October 18, 1897, they landed their boats on the side of the Klondike River opposite Dawson. Jack and his friends crossed the Klondike River and looked around for a place to pitch their tent. They saw a log cabin with a large open space alongside, so they asked the owners of the cabin for permission to camp. The answer was a quick yes.

The men in the cabin were two brothers, Louis and Marshall Bond, from Santa Clara, California, only about forty miles south of Oakland. The brothers — both about ten years older than Jack — came from a wealthy family. Their father, Judge Hiram G. Bond, owned a large ranch in Santa Clara and operated one of the banks in town.

Jack liked the Bond brothers very much. Later they corresponded occasionally, and after the Gold Rush — in mid-October 1901 — Jack spent a day visiting the Bond ranch in Santa Clara. He was impressed with the property: the spacious, twenty-five-room house had a roofed porch, or veranda, on three sides; a gravel driveway wound gracefully among high trees; an artesian well pumped cool water into a large tank the Bonds used for swimming; there were acres and acres of

*Marshall Bond (at far left) and the dog Jack (also at left),
the model for Buck in* The Call of the Wild

prune orchards; varieties of dogs scampered around the property.

In Dawson, Jack was very taken with one of the large dogs the Bond brothers had bought in Seattle on their way north. His name, coincidentally, was Jack, and he appeared to be a mixed breed — half St. Bernard and half collie. Jack London admired the combination of strength and gentleness in this dog. He was amazed when the animal one day pulled a sled loaded with one thousand pounds of firewood all by himself.

A few years later — in December 1902 — Jack London began writing one of his greatest books, *The Call of the Wild*. The hero of the story is a dog named

Buck. It is a mixed breed — St. Bernard and "Scotch shepherd dog" (or collie). Buck lives on a large ranch in Santa Clara owned by a judge. The ranch has a gravel driveway, a large house with a veranda, and a swimming tank. One night Buck is stolen by one of the workers on the ranch and sold to a man who sends him to Seattle to be trained as a sled dog for the Klondike. Buck travels by ship to Dyea, crosses the Chilkoot Pass, goes to Dawson City . . . in short, Buck in many ways shares the experiences that Jack London had in the Klondike.

Fred Thompson's diary abruptly ends the day that they met the Bond brothers, so for Jack's activities the rest of that Klondike winter we must depend upon his own comments later and upon letters and memoirs sent to Charmian London by his Northland companions after he died.

One of the men who knew Jack on the island that winter was W. B. "Bert" Hargrave. He wrote about the first time he entered Jack's cabin: "London was seated on the edge of a bunk, rolling a cigarette. He smoked incessantly. . . . One of his partners, Goodman, was preparing a meal, and the other, Sloper, was doing some carpentry work."

Hargrave recalled that after the chores were done, Jack and the others on the island spent their long, dark days doing about all they could do — talk. Jack would tell about his sailing and tramping adventures; he would argue about socialism; he would explain and defend the theories of human evolution he had been reading about. Jack always held his own in these debates, no matter how stiff the opposition. "One could not meet him," wrote Bert Hargrave, "without feeling the impact of a superior intellect."

All was not friendliness and happiness in the London cabin that winter. Fights were common among partners in the North. One man reported seeing two partners out on a lonely island in the middle of the Yukon River, punching each other in the face as hard as they could. Sometimes men became so angry with each other that they simply divided up their goods and went their own ways. Sometimes they were so enraged that they would do crazy things — like cut possessions in two so that each could have half. Jack once broke the blade of the favorite axe of his partner Merritt Sloper, who became so angry that it looked as if a fight would start any moment. But cooler heads stopped the battle before it began, and to keep the peace Jack decided to move into another cabin with B. F. "Doc" Harvey.

But for the most part, Jack always remembered his winter in the Yukon fondly. He made great friends. Although he found very little gold in the Klondike, the year brought him other riches. He met American Indians, North-west Mounted Police, travelers from all over the world. He learned about gold mining, about traveling by dog-team, about the dreary Yukon winter, about the bitter cold, about brave men and women and animals, and about the "white silence" — the awesome spectacle of snow and ice from horizon to horizon.

Late in January 1898, Jack traveled up Henderson Creek and stayed in a cabin built by a friend, Charley

Taylor. One day he carved a message in the wall: "Jack London Miner/Author Jan. 27, 1898." This so-called Jack London Cabin then lay virtually undisturbed for nearly seventy years. It wasn't until the mid-1960s that a man with the appropriate name of Dick North went by dog-team to the Henderson Creek region, looking for the cabin, which some trappers had told him was still standing.

On April 1, 1965, he found it. It is a small log structure, thirteen-by-thirteen feet, a single room. Trappers and hunters had apparently used it over the years, for there were signs of temporary occupants. The slab with Jack's writing had been cut away, however, by a souvenir hunter. But by 1969, the slab had been re-acquired and tested, and it fit perfectly into the cut in the wall of the cabin. Handwriting experts, however, do not agree that the writing is Jack's. Nevertheless, tourists today can see two Jack London cabins. One is in Oakland, the other in Dawson City. Both are exact replicas of the Henderson Creek cabin; both contain logs from the original.

Jack grew sick as spring arrived in the Yukon. He was suffering from scurvy, a disease caused by a lack of vitamin C. Because fresh fruit — a major source of the vitamin — was simply not available all winter, there were many in the North weakened by the disease. The symptoms are dreadful — swelling and bleeding gums, loosening teeth, dark spots on the skin, weakness, pains in the muscles and joints. Death occurs if the disease is not treated. Jack later made use of his personal

suffering to bring a harsh reality to some of his Northland stories. In one called "The Mistake of Creation,"
Smoke Bellew and Shorty find a mining camp where
everyone is dying from scurvy. And in another story,
"Finis," a man named Morgenson battles a severe case
of scurvy but dies before he can reach Dyea and help.

Despite his discomfort, Jack must have been
mightily impressed early in May by the spring breakup
of the Yukon River — one of the great sights in all of
nature. Loud cracking sounds sometimes echo across
the snow like rifle shots for hours before the actual
break. And during the breakup, the enormous pressure
of the river sometimes propels blocks of ice as large as
houses into the air and onto the shore. In one of Jack's
stories, "At the Rainbow's End," a man named Donald
is caught on an island in the river during breakup. He
climbs a tree to avoid the onrushing ice. But it is hopeless: "A great wall of white flung itself upon the island.
Trees, dogs, men, were blotted out, as though the hand
of God had wiped the face of nature clean. This much
he saw, then swayed an instant longer in his lofty perch
and hurtled far out into the frozen hell."

When the river was totally clear — probably in
early June that year — Jack and Doc Harvey dismantled their cabin, assembled the logs into a raft, and
floated down to Dawson City to sell the logs to the
sawmill. There was a tremendous demand for lumber in
town — for housing, for businesses, for mine shafts and
equipment. So Jack and Doc Harvey got a good price
for the logs — six hundred dollars. Jack apparently got

some treatment for his scurvy at the local hospital. They spent a few days looking around Dawson, whose population by this time had begun to swell and would, by midsummer, reach thirty thousand. At the height of the gold rush, Dawson would have theaters, banks, literary societies, stores and businesses of every variety, local telephone service, and a handful of millionaires who had struck it rich on the creeks. The town would brag that it was "the Paris of the North."

But Jack did not stay in Dawson long enough to see all this happen. He very much needed to get back to civilization and to fresh fruits and vegetables. On June 8, Jack, Charley Taylor, and John Thorson left Dawson City in a leaky homemade boat. That day Jack saw only a depressing sight: "dreary, desolate Dawson, built in a swamp, flooded to the second story, populated by dogs, mosquitoes and gold-seekers." They would float seventeen hundred miles, nearly the entire length of the Yukon River, to St. Michael on Alaska's western coast; from there they would take steamships home. During the first part of their journey, Jack kept some brief notes about his activities and seemed, at times, to be jotting down ideas he might use later in his writing.

Along the way, they passed the mining community of Fortymile — mostly abandoned; they passed the once-booming Circle City, but it too was almost deserted. They entered a long, dreary section of the river called the Yukon Flats and amused themselves by shooting geese. Twice they pulled into shore in the evening to watch American Indians dancing. They battled mosquitoes that swarmed about them thickly; Jack believed the pests actually cooperated with one another in their attacks. From the river they caught and ate luscious Chinook salmon.

On June 18, they arrived in Anvik, Alaska, where Jack acquired some vegetables for his scurvy. He wrote that the disease had "now almost entirely crippled me from my waist down. Right leg drawing up, can no longer straighten it, even in walking must put my whole weight on toes. These few raw potatoes and tomatoes are worth more to me than an Eldorado claim."

On June 30, they arrived in St. Michael early in the morning; Jack left that very day. His final comment in his diary indicates his mood: "Leave St. Michaels — unregrettable moment." He had no gold — except what remained from his sale of the cabin logs. He wrote later, "I brought back nothing from the Klondike but my scurvy."

Jack worked his way from Alaska to Vancouver, British Columbia, by shoveling coal on a steamship. From there he took another ship for San Francisco. When he crossed the bay to Oakland, he found that his mother was now living in another place only a few blocks away from their previous home. This was no surprise, of course; the Londons moved often. But there was a surprise waiting for Jack. A terrible one.

SIX

1898–1903: Loss, Luck, and a Dog Named Buck

Back in California a year later, recovering from scurvy, I found . . . that I was the head and the sole bread-winner of a household.

— Jack London, *John Barleycorn*

John London was dead.

This gentle, quiet man — the only man Jack would ever call "Father" — was dead at the age of seventy. On October 14, 1897, a day when Jack was prospecting on Henderson Creek in the Yukon, his father died of heart problems and lung disease back in Oakland. Two days later he was buried in Mountain View Cemetery.

After hearing the news Jack left Oakland almost immediately. Although he knew that he now had important family responsibilities, he wanted to get away. He needed to think. What would his father's death mean for his own future? Would a writing career be possible now? With his recent gold-mining experiences, he wanted to try his hand at a new strike in the nearby mountains of Nevada. A profitable gold claim would give his family the financial security they had never had. Maybe he would get lucky. . . .

He didn't. In a letter to his friend Ted Applegarth

on September 13, he wrote: "Right after my arrival I was off to the mountains on a prospecting trip and have but recently returned, *sans* [without] result." He must have realized then that gold mining was far too risky and un-predictable an occupation — especially when there were people who now needed him more than ever.

Jack was truly the head of a household. Although Flora could still bring in a little money with her piano lessons, sewing, and séances, it was not enough to sup-port her, six-year-old Johnny Miller (the son of John London's daughter Ida), and Jack himself.

But the economy was no better than it had been when Jack left for the Klondike. "Times were hard," he wrote. "I had no thought of career. That was over and done with. I had to find food for two mouths beside my own and keep a roof over our heads."

He registered with employment bureaus, applied in person for numerous jobs, checked with employed friends and acquaintances, and placed ads in three newspapers. Nothing. Finally, desperate for cash, he was forced to pawn three items of great personal value to him: the bicycle Eliza had bought him, the silver watch that his brother-in-law had given him in Alaska, and a mackintosh (raincoat) that had belonged to John London — the only item his father had left to him.

He continued to apply for all sorts of jobs. "I tried to become a studio model," he recalled, "but there were too many fine-bodied young fellows out of jobs. I an-swered advertisements of elderly invalids in need of companions. And I almost became a sewing machine agent [salesman], on commission, without salary. . . . I mowed lawns, trimmed hedges, took up carpets, beat them, and laid them again."

Jack decided to take an examination for a job in the Postal Service. He knew that he would probably do well on the test, and although he was not excited about a career as a mail carrier, he very much needed a steady job and an income his family could depend on. On October 1, 1898, he took the test. He would have to wait more than two months for the results.

He had not yet given up his dream of being a writer. In the free moments he could steal, usually very late at night, he was still writing and mailing away his stories and articles. But he was not having any success at all. On September 17 he sent an inquiry to the *San Francisco Bulletin*: Would they like to see a piece he had written about his recent trip down the Yukon River? Jack tried to sell himself in the letter, to show the editor that he was both experienced and capable. "I have sailed and traveled quite extensively in other parts of the world and have learned to seize upon that which is interesting, to grasp the true romance of things, and to understand the people I may be thrown against."

But the editor was not persuaded. At the bottom of Jack's letter, he wrote: "Interest in Alaska has subsided in an amazing degree. Then, again, so much has been written, that I do not think it would pay us to buy your story." In later years, when Jack was selling his

Northland stories and articles to magazines and news-papers and book publishers all over the world, this editor would be proved completely wrong.

Throughout September and October, Jack contin-ued to send poems, essays, and short stories to many different magazines without success. He even tried writing and selling jokes.

About this time he received bad news of another sort: Fred Jacobs — his friend from Oakland High School who had tutored him in chemistry and physics for his entrance examinations to Berkeley — had died of a fever on the way to the Philippines. He had gone there to work aboard a hospital ship in the Spanish-American War. Jack was calm and philosophical about the loss of his friend. "So be it," he wrote to Ted Ap-plegarth. "He has only solved the mystery a little quicker than the rest of us."

Early in December 1898, Frederick Irons Bamford, the Oakland librarian, joined with a few others to es-tablish the Ruskin Club. Jack was one of the charter members, and frequently attended the monthly meet-ings until the club disbanded eight years later. The club was named in honor of English essayist and artist John Ruskin (1819–1900), whose ideas about art, literature, and politics were very controversial. The meetings fea-tured lectures, debates, and discussions of great interest to Jack — especially when the topic was socialism. Jack sometimes led the meetings — or read his own essays to the group. The Ruskin Club became yet another way for Jack to continue his education outside of school.

Jack was still seeing and corresponding with Mabel Applegarth, though their relationship had not developed the way he had once wanted it to. She often seemed more interested in changing him than in supporting his dream to be a writer.

Shortly before Jack had left for the Yukon, the Applegarths had moved to College Park, California, a small community nestled between San Jose and Santa Clara, about forty-five miles south of San Francisco. Jack occasionally visited the Applegarths there, either riding his bike — when it was not in the pawnshop — or taking the train. The little College Park depot, only a couple of blocks from the Applegarths' home, is the station in *The Call of the Wild* where Buck begins his journey to the Northland.

Jack's letters to Mabel in late 1898 are full of his frustrations — with his life, with his relationships, and at times with Mabel herself. Once he wrote sharply to her: "I do appreciate your interest in my affairs, but — we have no common ground. In a general, vaguely general, way, you know my aspirations; but of the real Jack, his thoughts, feelings, etc., you are positively ignorant. Yet, little as you do know, you know more about me than any body else. I have fought and am fighting my battle alone."

In early December he wrote to Mabel about a small success with his writing. The *Overland Monthly*, a San Francisco magazine, had accepted one of his Northland stories, "To the Man on Trail," and would publish it in January. They would pay him five dollars.

Jack had been hoping for more money. But the *Overland Monthly* was an important magazine. And five dollars was a week's salary for many people in 1898–1899. He would use part of the money to retrieve some of his items from the pawnbroker.

The week between Christmas 1898 and New Year's Day 1899 was one of the bleakest in Jack's life. On Christmas morning he wrote a sad letter to Mabel, calling it "about the loneliest Christmas I ever faced." He could not afford his January fee for his rented typewriter, which would mean his chances with publishers would be reduced even more, since they did not like handwritten articles and stories. He was terribly depressed. He had come to believe that success is really just luck. "The whole thing is a gamble," he wrote, "and those least fitted to understand the game win the most." And on New Year's Eve he wrote to Ted, admitting to his friend: "I have never been so hard up in my life." The same day he also wrote to Mabel once again, this time revealing that he had pawned his bicycle and "other articles too numerous to mention." He enclosed a copy of the *Overland Monthly* that contained his story and mentioned that it took a borrowed dime to buy it for her.

In the New Year of 1899 things did not immediately improve. Mabel did not write to him on his twenty-third birthday, January 12, and he scolded her in a letter of his own on the thirteenth: "I doubt if you can understand how disappointed I have been — thirteen days since I wrote you, and no sign."

On January 28 he wrote with better news: he had finally heard about his test score for the post office job. He had earned the highest score. As soon as there was an opening, he would have first chance at it. He would make forty-five dollars a month for six months, then move to sixty-five. It would seem like a fortune for the little family.

But then the *Overland Monthly* told Jack they would pay him $7.50 per story for all he could send them. This, too, was steady income. But how many stories would the magazine really publish? Wouldn't accepting the mail-delivery job be a more responsible thing to do? Now he hoped that the job offer wouldn't come too soon. Maybe he would be able to succeed as a writer after all. Maybe he could turn the job down . . . if he could just make a little more money, just a little more.

By now, many of his possessions were in the pawnshop. He was spending virtually all his money on paper, stamps, envelopes. Late into the night he would study the work of other writers. Why had they succeeded? In what ways were their stories better than his? He went to the Oakland Public Library and pored over the most recent magazines. What worked? How could he change his own writing so that the editors would buy it?

He studied a little book about writing by Herbert Spencer called *Philosophy of Style*. From Spencer he learned to keep his writing simple and direct. "The more simple and the better arranged its parts," advised Spencer, "the greater will be the effect produced." Jack thought this made sense. Spencer also cautioned against using too many long, unfamiliar words. Writers should employ exact, precise words.

Jack was nearly fanatic about learning new words. Whenever he heard or read words he did not know, he wrote them on slips of paper and hung them around his room. He carried them in his coat pockets, glancing at them whenever he could. Each new word, he said, is "one more new sharp-edged tool ready to your hand and to your service."

One of the most popular writers in Jack London's day was Rudyard Kipling, an Englishman whose *Just So Stories* and *The Jungle Book* continue to be favorites with readers today. But Kipling also wrote rugged adventure stories that were praised by readers and critics on both sides of the Atlantic. So Jack — hoping to learn from Kipling — examined his work closely. He even copied by hand some of Kipling's stories so that he could "feel" the sentences that the Englishman had written. After a while he began to catch on to how Kipling put words and sentences together — how Kipling *thought*.

None of this brought money into the family. And just when Jack was at his lowest — just when, once again, he might have had to give up — a letter came from the editor of the *Black Cat*, an Eastern short-story magazine. The editor, H. D. Umbstaetter, liked his story "A Thousand Deaths," although he called it "more lengthy than strengthy." The magazine offered him forty dollars for it if he would grant permission for them to cut it by half. *Grant permission?* Jack nearly laughed aloud. "I told Mr. Umbstaetter he could cut it down two-halves if he'd only send the money along. He did, by return mail."

The thin envelope arrived on February 23. Later, Jack wrote what that forty-dollar check meant to him: "I was at the end of my tether, beaten out, starved, ready to go back to coal shoveling or ahead to suicide. . . . I was finished — finished as only a very young, very sick, and very hungry young man could be. . . . I would never write again." It was Umbstaetter, wrote Jack, who "made me possible" and "saved my literary life."

His first stop after cashing the check was the pawnshop. "I got my bicycle, my watch, and my father's mackintosh . . . and rented a typewriter." He also paid off some bills to some local grocers. For the first and one of the only times in his life he was free of debts. He was making a living as a writer — not a great living, but a living.

Then came the news from the post office. An opening was available.

Jack was torn: if he took the job, he knew he would not have the time to do the writing he wanted to do. Carrying the mail would be tiring. He knew what happened to his mind when he worked at hard physical labor — the power plant and the laundry had taught him that. Yet if he turned it down, wouldn't he be denying his family the steady, reliable income they so desperately needed?

He decided to approach the postmaster directly, explain his dilemma. Maybe he would understand, would let Jack pass up this particular job and, if the writing was not paying enough, take the next one that came along. In *John Barleycorn* Jack tells what happened:

> I frankly told him the situation. It looked as if I might win out at writing. The chance was good, but not certain. Now, if he would pass me by and select the next man on the eligible list, and give me a call at the next vacancy –
>
> But he shut me off with: "Then you don't want the position?"
>
> "But I do," I protested. "Don't you see, if you will pass me over this time – "
>
> "If you want it you will take it," he said coldly.
>
> Happily for me, the cursed brutality of the man made me angry.
>
> "Very well," I said. "I won't take it."

Jack had decided. He would be a writer — a "brain merchant," as he called it. He felt he was close to success.

Shortly after "To the Man on Trail" and "The White Silence" appeared in the *Overland Monthly*, Jack received a flattering letter from another aspiring young writer named Cloudesley Johns. "What an encouragement your short note was!" replied Jack. "It's the first word of cheer I have received (a cheer, far more potent than publishers' checks)." The two would become fast friends and would exchange hundreds of letters and numerous visits.

In these letters to his friend, Jack revealed vital information about the early years of his career. He even told what he looked like. Johns once wrote to ask for a photograph, and Jack responded with a self-portrait in words:

> Stand five foot seven or eight in stocking feet – sailor life shortened me. At present time weight 168 lbs; but readily jump same pretty close to 180 when I take up outdoor life and go to roughing it. Am clean shaven – when I let 'em come, blonde moustache and black whiskers – but they don't come long. Clean face makes my age enigmatical; and equally competent judges variously estimate my age from twenty to thirty. Greenish-grey eyes, heavy brows which meet; brown hair, which, by the way, was black when I was born, then came out during an infantile sickness and returned positively white – so white that . . . [Jennie Prentiss] called me "Cotton Ball." Face bronzed through many long-continued liaisons with the sun, though just now, owing to bleaching process of sedentary life, it is positively yellow. Several

```
scars – hiatus of eight front upper teeth,
usually disguised with false plate.
There I am. . . .
```

Jack also hammered out in these letters his beliefs about many things — from relationships with women, to politics, to what good writing ought to be. In one letter, in particular, Jack practically shouted from the page what he believed about writing:

```
Don't you tell the reader. Don't. Don't.
Don't. But HAVE YOUR CHARACTERS TELL IT
BY THEIR DEEDS, ACTIONS, TALK, ETC. . . .
And get the atmosphere. Get the breadth
and thickness to your stories, and not
only the length . . . PUT ALL THOSE THINGS
WHICH ARE YOURS INTO THE STORIES, INTO
THE TALES, ELIMINATING YOURSELF . . . AND
THIS WILL BE THE ATMOSPHERE. AND THIS
ATMOSPHERE WILL BE YOU, DON'T YOU UNDER-
STAND, YOU! YOU! YOU! . . . Don't narrate –
paint! draw! build! – CREATE!
```

Throughout the winter and spring of 1899 Jack continued to work hard at his writing — and at his education. By now he had established a routine that he maintained for the rest of his life. He would spend his mornings writing — always trying to produce a thousand to fifteen hundred words in his longhand scrawl, filling up sheet after sheet of paper. "I have made it a rule," he wrote to Cloudesley Johns, "to make up next day what I fall behind; but when I run ahead, to not permit it to count on the following day."

The rest of the day he would laboriously pound his rented typewriter, transferring his stories and articles into the typewritten copies he would mail to his publishers. He would then write letters — to friends and editors and other correspondents. And, of course, he would spend many hours per day reading and study-

Cloudesley Johns, Jack's first fan and long-time friend

ing, far into the night, getting by on only a few hours' sleep. Jack had strong self-discipline, and because of it he was able to stick to this routine no matter where he was or how he felt — sailing, camping, sick or well. And because of this he was able in a short lifetime to produce a large body of work. "I am a believer in regular work," he wrote, "and never wait for inspiration."

But success was not coming very fast. His small checks from the *Overland Monthly* were not enough to support the family — especially when he needed so much cash for writing paper, ink, stamps, envelopes. Flora had a small pension from the government because of John London's wartime disability, and her other activities brought in a little, but they were barely getting by. Something needed to happen — and soon.

Throughout the summer his stories continued to appear, one per month, in the *Overland Monthly*, and in late July he decided to take a break from his strict routine. He chose the cheapest form of transportation he could: his bicycle. It would be his first real vacation since he had gone to Yosemite with the Applegarths several years earlier. He and a friend left home on their bikes, rode to the Oakland ferry depot, steamed across to San Francisco, then pedaled south about thirty-five miles to Stanford University near Palo Alto. (He would never know, of course, that about ninety years later Stanford University would publish his complete letters and short stories in six large volumes.)

From Stanford, they had planned to travel south another fifteen miles to College Park to visit the Applegarths. They would then pedal on into San Jose, only a few miles more south, ride to the observatory at Mt. Hamilton, then cycle up the length of the east side of the Bay, about fifty miles, back to Oakland. It was just what Jack needed: a break from all his work, some hard exercise to strengthen his softening body, a visit with good friends. But his bad luck would not change: "Trip knocked out in the middle," he wrote crisply to Cloudesley Johns. "Whole lot of company came to our house. . . ." It would be late September before he could finally get away.

During the summer of 1899 he was working hard to find publishers for two of his projects. One, a short story, "An Odyssey of the North," he had sent to one of the most important magazines in America, *The Atlantic Monthly*. This Boston-based magazine — still in business today — published only the best work by the best writers in the country. To be accepted by *The Atlantic* was an honor Jack had dreamed of — the magazine represented the respectable literary world he wanted so much to inhabit. He was also trying to place his first book, a collection of nine of his Klondike stories, most of which had already been published in the *Overland Monthly*.

In late July, — when he had planned to be on his bicycle trip — he received a thin letter from the *Atlantic*. Thin envelopes, he knew, were usually good news. They contained checks. Or acceptances. The thick envelopes held his returned manuscripts — and a rejection slip.

The *Atlantic* liked his story! They would publish it if he would cut three thousand of its thirteen thousand words. And they would pay him $120 — by far the most he had ever received for something he had written. Jack was ecstatic. His work would appear alongside that of writers far more famous — with far more schooling. Thousands of people all over the country would read him, would know his name. It was a staggering success.

His collection of stories was not faring so well. The Macmillan Company in New York was not interested. So he sent it to Houghton Mifflin Company in Boston, another large publishing house. And waited.

At the end of October he wrote to Johns: "Have heard nothing more concerning my collection. They do take their time about it." It was frustrating, all this waiting. But some of his articles and stories were slowly starting to sell. Every now and then he would receive small checks — twenty-five dollars here, five dollars there. It was helping. He even received a twenty-five-dollar surprise from *Youth's Companion*, a magazine for children. He splurged and bought a new bicycle.

And then on November 1 came the greatest news of all: Houghton Mifflin would publish his book of Klondike stories. The entire book would bear the title of one of the stories: *The Son of the Wolf*. The story is about a rough Northland prospector named "Scruff" Mackenzie who has spent two years "groping for the gold . . . in the shadow of the Arctic Circle." He is lonely and decides he will take a wife. So he hitches up his dogs and heads straight into an encampment of American Indians in the remote Tanana River region. He spies the chief's daughter, Zarinska, and decides she will be his mate. The American Indians are shocked at his boldness. They threaten his life. But Mackenzie defeats them with arguments, and he defeats some of them in hand-to-hand combat. Zarinska willingly leaves with him, and the members of the tribe recognize that Mackenzie is a natural force too powerful to resist. He is "the son of the wolf."

Jack signed the book contract on December 25 — quite a Christmas present. Then a few days later he rode to College Park to spend the rest of the holidays with Ted and Mabel Applegarth.

For the next couple of years success began to arrive at Jack's door as regularly as failure had visited in the years before. Like Scruff Mackenzie, he had proved his worth in an alien world — the world of learning and literature, a world far different from the one he had known as a child.

Jack's luck had turned with the century. When the New Year dawned on 1900, his days of poverty were finally over. He wrote every day, and much of what he wrote he was now able to sell. His production between 1900 and 1902 was astonishing.

In 1900 *The Son of the Wolf* and about thirty other articles and stories were published in many important magazines and newspapers around the country. For some he received fifty dollars and even more. Another major book publisher agreed to pay him $125 per month for five months if he would write a novel for them (it appeared in 1902). In 1901 *The God of His Fathers* (another collection of Klondike stories) was published, plus another twenty-five articles and stories appeared in magazines. And 1902 publications included *A Daughter of the Snows* (the Klondike novel he had contracted to write in 1900), *Children of the Frost* (more Klondike stories), *The Cruise of the "Dazzler"* (a novel for young people based on his oyster pirate days), and a couple of dozen magazine pieces.

With his publishing success came offers of other

kinds. Newspapers wanted him to write stories for them, and clubs and societies all over the Bay Area wanted him to speak at their meetings. The Oakland Socialist Democratic Party, recognizing him as a local celebrity, urged him to become more active in socialist politics, and in 1901 he was their candidate for mayor of Oakland. He did not campaign much, and the local newspapers did not take him seriously. The *San Francisco Evening Post* joked that if he won, he would probably change Oakland's name to "London" — or maybe "Jacktown." Winning, of course, was never a serious possibility — Jack received only 245 votes. But the publicity helped the sales of his books.

In 1902 Jack embarked on two major writing projects that show the wide range of his interests and talents. The first began almost as an accident. In July he had agreed to go to South Africa for the American Press Association to cover the aftermath of the Boer War. *Boor* is the Dutch word for farmer. In South Africa many of the Dutch were fearful of the increasing presence of Great Britain in the region — especially when gold was discovered. The war, which had begun in 1899, had officially ended a couple of months before Jack was asked to interview some of the participants.

When he arrived in New York City, he learned that the people he was to interview had scattered. The press association canceled his trip. In a letter from New York to a friend, Jack wrote that he was "grievously disappointed." But he decided to turn the situation to his advantage. He convinced the press association to let him go to England instead and begin a project very near to his heart and personal history. He would disguise himself as one of the homeless poor of the East End of London. He would live among them, experience on the streets what they experienced, and then — in the evenings — write a book about his observations. The association would arrange for publications of pieces of this book in a magazine. The association agreed, and some installments of his book, called *The People of the Abyss*, appeared in *Wilshire's Magazine* between March of 1903 and January 1904.

Although he did not have a publisher lined up to bring out the entire book, he was now confident enough in his work to know he would not have a problem once he completed it. On July 30, 1902, he sailed aboard the steamship *Majestic* to Liverpool, England. He arrived August 6, and was at work by the sixteenth. He was staggered by the poverty and the hopelessness he saw. It was worse — far worse — than what he had seen in the lower reaches of America. "The whole thing," he wrote to a friend, "all the conditions of life, the intensity of it, everything is overwhelming. I never conceived such a mass of misery in the world before." As usual, he kept a strict schedule of writing each day. By September 28 — after a fierce routine of living on the streets and writing — he announced happily in a letter: "The book is finished!"

He then traveled around Europe for about a month — a trip he never wrote very much about. On November 5 he returned aboard the *Teutonic* to New

York City where he met with George P. Brett, president of the Macmillan Company, a major American book and magazine publisher. The company had already brought out Jack's book *Children of the Frost*, and he hoped to convince Brett to publish *The People of the Abyss*.

Brett was interested — in fact, he was interested in more than just this single book. He was thinking that he would love to sign this rising young star to an exclusive contract with Macmillan. Jack was interested. It would mean a regular income, and the end of frustrating searches for places to publish his books. When he was back in California and finally sent the entire manuscript of *Abyss* to New York, he included a long letter to Brett outlining a financial arrangement. "If you would find it practicable to advance me $150 per month for one year . . . ," Jack proposed, "I guarantee to have in your hands *The Flight of the Duchess* and *The Mercy of the Sea* by December 1st, 1903. In addition, I shall by that time have completed two other books which are now nearly done."

Brett was willing. But he wanted a two-year deal for six books. He wanted Jack to write more slowly, more carefully. Jack agreed. On December 11, 1902, he signed the contract. But he never wrote *The Flight of the Duchess*, a California story; nor did he write *The Mercy of the Sea*, an account of his seal-hunting voyage aboard the *Sophia Sutherland*. Instead, about a week before he signed with Macmillan, he began working on something else — something he referred to simply as "an animal story."

Jack started this story on the first of December 1902, and by the time he finished it on January 26, it had grown to about thirty-two thousand words — quite a bit more than he had originally intended. It was no longer a short story. It was a short novel, or novella. He mailed it to Philadelphia to the *Saturday Evening Post*, one of the most popular weekly magazines in the country. As he later wrote, the *Post* liked it, "for they snapped it up right away." They offered him $750 and would publish it in five installments in the summer. The *Post* asked him to cut five thousand words — which he did as soon as he accepted their offer.

Jack was proud of the tale, and when he wrote to George Brett to try to interest Macmillan in bringing it out as a book, he said that it was "utterly different in subject and treatment from the rest of the animal stories which have been so successful." He wasn't sure about a title, though. He thought, maybe, he might name it something like . . . *The Call of the Wild?*

The first person to read the book at Macmillan was G. R. Carpenter, a professor of English at Columbia University in New York. Carpenter often read manuscripts for Macmillan. He was able to screen out ones that were not suitable. But in the case of *The Call of the Wild*, Carpenter had very little negative to say: "The style is," he wrote, "remarkably good."

Brett loved the novel. He called it "pretty perfect

as it is" and did not want Jack to make many changes — except to remove some of the swearing. He was afraid that parents and children's librarians would not buy the book if there was too much rough language in it. Jack and Brett did some quibbling about the title. At one point Jack suggested *The Sleeping Wolf* or *The Wolf* — titles which neither of them really liked. Eventually, they settled on its current one.

Brett made an offer that would end up costing Jack millions of dollars. Jack was still not well known around the country as a novelist. His only other novel, *A Daughter of the Snows*, had been, everyone agreed, a failure. So Brett suggested a deal: Macmillan would publish *The Call of the Wild* in an expensive, well-illustrated edition. They would advertise it heavily. They would send copies to book reviewers all over the country. They would, in other words, spend a small fortune to promote the book. Doing this, said Brett, would create a better market for all of Jack's books to follow. For his part, Jack would accept a one-time payment of two thousand dollars. He would not receive any author's royalties — usually ten percent of the book's sales. Jack agreed quickly. "I am sure," he replied to Brett, "that pushing the book in the manner you mention will be of the utmost value to me. . . ."

The Call of the Wild has been one of the best-selling books in American literary history. It has been in print continuously since 1903. Today more than twenty different companies publish the book in English alone. It has been translated into dozens of other languages and is popular everywhere. Millions of students read it in school every year. It sits on the shelf in bookshops all over the world.

Yet all Jack London ever received for this, his most popular book, was $2,750. There is no question that in the 1990s the book earns more than that every single day. But Jack never expressed any anger — or even regret — about his decision. For Macmillan stuck to its part of the bargain. The volume was published in a beautiful form — lushly illustrated on thick, creamy paper. The company sent hundreds of copies to book reviewers, and all of them wrote powerfully positive reviews of the book. Some called it the best dog story ever written. Others called it a masterpiece — a strong new novel from the most original and exciting new voice in American writing. In only a few weeks it was on best-seller lists.

A reputation was made. Never again in his lifetime would anyone wonder who Jack London was. Never again would a publisher dismiss him as an unknown, undereducated writer. He had become an international celebrity, a success beyond his wildest dreams. He had made it.

SEVEN

1900–1905: Friends and Lovers

You know I do things quickly. Sunday
morning, last, I had not the slightest
intention of doing what I am going to
do. I came down and looked over the
house I was to move into — that
fathered the thought. I made up my
mind. Sunday evening I opened transac-
tions for a wife; by Monday evening had
the affair well under way; and next
Saturday morning I shall marry. . . .

— Jack London, letter to Netta Eames,
the *Overland Monthly*, April 3, 1900

While Jack was struggling to establish himself as a writer, he was certainly not neglecting his social life. He had a large group of friends and, before he decided to marry, several romantic involvements with women.

Mabel Applegarth was the first woman to occupy his romantic imagination for a long period of time. He met her while he was in high school, and he continued his relationship with her for a couple of years. But at some point — perhaps while he was in the Klondike — he began to realize that she was not right for him. His passion for her cooled. "I awoke," he wrote later, ". . . and my puppy love was over." He remained friends with the Applegarths. He continued to visit them and to write a few letters. But that was all.

In the fall of 1899 another woman entered Jack's life. It began in San Francisco at a lecture — always one of his favorite activities. The lectures charged no fee for admission — so it was another inexpensive way to educate himself. In the audience that night was Anna Strunsky, a student at Stanford University who was two years younger than he. Jack was introduced to

Anna Strunsky, an early love

her and was smitten. She was very beautiful, highly intelligent — and because she was a Russian Jew, even somewhat mysterious and exotic.

In December, Jack began writing a flurry of letters to her, courting her with his powerful, persuasive words. In the first few letters, he addressed her as "Miss Strunsky." He confessed to feeling clumsy around her and tried to impress her with his knowledge of literature. He offered to help her with her own writing — "believe me sincerely at your service," he wrote. He was thrilled to learn she would be transferring to the University of California at nearby Berkeley — an easy bike ride for him, not the thirty-five miles or so separating him from Stanford.

He bluntly wrote how he wanted to see her again. "Take me this way: a stray guest, a bird of passage, splashing with salt-rimed [covered] wings through a brief moment of your life — a rude and blundering bird, used to large airs and great spaces." After writing such passionate letters to her for a month, he finally found the courage to address her as "Anna" instead of "Miss Strunsky."

"There!" he wrote. "Let's get our friendship down to a comfortable basis." He said that calling her "Miss Strunsky" was as unpleasant to him as wearing a stiff white collar. He continued to write to her throughout the winter and spring of 1900. They were recommending books to each other, and sharing ideas about writing. Jack was giving her his work to read and criticize. They were having fun. But Anna's affections were accelerating more slowly than Jack's. Although there is no doubt that she loved him, she was not ready to make a permanent commitment.

And so on April 7 — the same day that *The Son of the Wolf* was published in Boston — Jack abruptly and unexpectedly married Bessie Maddern. Anna wrote to congratulate him. He admitted: "It was rather sudden. I always do things that way."

Bessie May Maddern was born July 13, 1876, almost exactly six months after Jack. The daughter of a plumber in Oakland, she was, according to their daughter, "slender and athletic, with vigorous, blue-black

Bessie Maddern London, Jack's first wife

hair and hazel eyes." Bessie was a serious and thought-ful young woman. Photographs rarely show her smiling. Jack had known her since 1896, when she had helped him study for the entrance examinations to the University of California, and she had been a friend ever since. She had been engaged to marry Jack's friend Fred Jacobs, but he had died in 1898. She was making a living by tutoring young students who were not able to attend school regularly.

On the night of Jack's decision, Bessie was visiting him at his house. While Jack was reading, Bessie and his stepsister Eliza were arranging his books on some new shelves. Eliza said later that his eyes suddenly appeared "to fill with visions, and he dropped his face and lay still for a long time." The idea, like a flash flood, had arrived without warning; in moments it filled his mind and imagination. As soon as Eliza left, Jack persuaded Bessie to marry him. He told her he did not love her, but it would be a good arrangement for them both. She would have a husband and father for their children; he would have a companion — and perhaps more.

Five months earlier Jack had written to Cloudes-ley Johns about all his frustrations with having to type his manuscripts. "When I get married," he joked, "guess I'll have to marry a type-writer girl. I do most heartily hate the job." But was he joking?

Jack's friends were shocked at his quick decision. Johns sent two quick notes. The first said only: "Jesus H. Christ!" In the second he wrote that he would withhold his congratulations for ten years. Perhaps the marriage would last that long.

Jack's mother, Flora, was stunned as well. Shortly before his marriage, Jack had moved to another house in Oakland only blocks away. But this one was a larger, two-story home with seven rooms. It was far more space than he had ever had. And he needed it. His routines of writing and studying demanded more room. Flora was still living with him, as was Johnny Miller, his nephew. Flora was excited at first. She would finally have a larger, more impressive house to manage. But Jack's marriage changed that. Suddenly, she was now a guest.

Within a few months, Jack's income permitted him to pay for another place for Flora and Johnny — a small cottage just behind his property.

On January 15, 1901, Bessie gave birth to a daughter. When he learned that his child was a girl, Jack was at first disappointed. He even referred to her as "It" for a couple of days. But it was not long before he and Bessie agreed on a name, and within weeks he was proudly writing to friends about being a father. To Anna, he wrote, "I have happiness in Joan — great, wonderful, glorious Joan."

Jack's marriage to Bessie and the birth of Joan did not change his interest in Anna Strunsky — now they were working together on a project. In 1900 they had developed the idea of publishing a book of letters — a fictional correspondence between two characters,

Jennie Prentiss, Jack's nurse, here pictured with Joan London

Dane Kempton (a Stanford professor) and his foster son, Herbert Wace (a student of economics at Berkeley). Jack would be Wace; Anna would be Kempton.

All the letters would be on the subject of love. Jack (as Wace) would see love as something to think about scientifically. He would argue that you could pick a wife as you would pick out a house — logically, sensibly. Anna (as Kempton) would be a romantic and would argue that love resides in the heart, not the mind.

They called the book *The Kempton-Wace Letters*, and they worked on it, off and on, for about three years. This required that they correspond frequently and that they meet from time to time. Jack found that his affection for Anna was deepening, despite his marriage to Bessie. Some of his letters to her began "Dear, dear Anna," and "Dear, dear You." In one letter in June 1902, he blurted out: "I am sick with love for you and need of you." From the tone and content of these letters it is clear that Anna was responding in kind. She and Jack had established a relationship that had serious consequences for his marriage and family.

But while Jack was in England, Anna learned that Bessie was pregnant. Anna was shocked. Hadn't Jack assured her that he and Bessie were all but finished? She wrote a sharp letter to him, effectively ending their romantic involvement. In 1906 she married William English Walling, a wealthy socialist, and gradually disappeared from Jack's life.

On October 20, 1902, the Londons had their second child, Bess, almost always called Becky. At this time, Jack and his family were living in a bungalow up in the Piedmont Hills overlooking Oakland. He loved this new place, as he wrote enthusiastically to Cloudesley Johns: "We have a big living room, every inch of it, floor and ceiling, finished in redwood. We could put the floor space of almost four cottages . . . into this one living room alone." The five-acre property, surrounded by fields of flowers, also had a small cottage where Flora and Johnny Miller lived. The view was spectacular. They could see, he wrote, "all of San Francisco Bay for a sweep of thirty or forty miles, and all the opposing shores such as San Francisco, Marin County and

Mount Tamalpais (to say nothing of the Golden Gate and the Pacific Ocean) — and all for $35.00 per month."

Jack had many friends, and as soon as he became well known in the Bay Area, had become the center of a very large group of writers, artists, and socialists. They were known as "The Crowd." To this ever-widening circle of friends, the Londons opened their new home on Wednesday afternoons and evenings — sometimes Sundays as well.

One of the most important of Jack's friends had entered his life early in his career. Herman "Jim" Whitaker was about ten years older and was in Oakland helping the socialists operate a cooperative grocery store. While Jack was still in high school, Whitaker invited him to join the Socialist Democratic Party. The two became great friends, and Whitaker taught the younger man to fence and box. Jack knew how to fight, of course. But it was this older friend who tamed the wildcat and taught him the science of boxing.

Frank Strawn-Hamilton was a hobo and socialist. Like Jack, he had been in jail for vagrancy. But for Strawn-Hamilton it was a regular event — he was convicted as many as thirty times. He lived on the streets, studied philosophy in the public library, and preached socialism and evolution to whoever would listen. Jack had first heard him speaking in the City Hall Park in Oakland and had been mesmerized by him. The two spent many hours together — it was probably Strawn-Hamilton who introduced Jack to Anna Strunsky.

Jack's best friend, however, was a poet, George Sterling. He was about eight years older than Jack and had moved from his native New York to California in 1890 to work in a real-estate office. He married Caroline "Carrie" Rand in 1896 and met Jack in 1901. Sterling had read Jack's story "The White Silence" and very much wanted to meet this young author who was causing so much excitement in the Bay Area.

He and Jack were very different — physically and otherwise. Sterling was tall and thin and serious. Jack was none of these. Sterling wanted to be a poet like the great poets of the past. Jack wanted to be a new kind of writer, a writer for today. And yet the two could not have been better friends. Jack called him "Greek" because of his friend's interests in ancient Greece — and because of his classical looks. Sterling called Jack "Wolf." These are the names they used to address and sign their many, many letters to each other. Sterling often proofread Jack's books for him, and Jack read Sterling's poems and offered suggestions.

The Crowd, however, was not a fixed group of friends. People came and went. Sometimes there were dozens of people at the Londons', sometimes only a handful. But there was always lots of laughter, drink, reading of new stories and poems, and discussions about exciting new ideas.

There were also physical activities. Jack had always been an active athlete and was fiercely competitive. He especially enjoyed cycling, boxing, and fencing, as well as such field events as broad and high jumping, putting the shot, and tossing a long, heavy pole called a caber. He also delighted The Crowd by walking on his hands.

One of the people who joined these gatherings from time to time was a young woman named Charmian Kittredge. Jack had first met her in 1900 when Netta Eames, Charmian's aunt and foster

Charmian Kittredge, who would become Jack's second wife, in 1898

mother, had interviewed him for an article she was writing in the *Overland Monthly*. Jack was immediately attracted to Charmian. He wrote to Cloudesley Johns that she was "a charming girl who writes book reviews, and who possesses a pretty little library wherein I have found all the late [recent] books which the public libraries are afraid to have circulate." By the middle of 1903, on the eve of the publication of *The Call of the Wild*, they were rapidly becoming something more than "just friends."

Clara Charmian Kittredge was born to Daisy and Willard "Kitt" Kittredge in California on November 27, 1871. She was about four years older than Jack. Her childhood — like Jack's — was not really a happy or secure one. Her mother was not well, so Charmian was passed from relative to relative. When she was about six, her mother died. Within a few months she was living with Netta Eames, her mother's married sister in Oakland. Here Charmian grew up in a household rich in books, music, and art. Later, her uncle taught her typing and shorthand. At sixteen, she enrolled at Mills Seminary and College, a school for young women. For two years she supported herself by serving as a secretary to Susan Mills, the owner and principal of the school.

Mills emphasized "book learning," of course, but the school also required students to participate in many physical activities. It was at Mills that Charmian learned to love all kinds of sports — swimming, diving, cycling, hiking, and horseback riding, her favorite. In the 1890s Charmian would not ride sidesaddle, which was the "proper" way for women to ride. This was shocking to the prim residents of Oakland, who considered Charmian something of a rebel — maybe worse.

After two years, she left Mills and went to work in San Francisco as a secretary. But soon she inherited some money from her father and uncle, so she was able to leave her job and enjoy a kind of security and comfort she had never known before. When her Aunt Netta and Netta's husband, Roscoe Eames, became involved with the publication of the *Overland Monthly* magazine, Charmian participated as well, writing book reviews and reading manuscripts that writers sent to the magazine — writers like Jack London.

When Netta interviewed Jack in the magazine offices in January 1900, Charmian saw him briefly for the first time. She was not much impressed: "a rather odd caller, clad in shabby bicycle trousers and dark gray woolen shirt. A nondescript tie, soft bicycle shoes, and a worn cap in one hand. There was a hasty introduction in the dim hall. . . . Then the apparently abashed young fellow ran lightly down the steps, pulling the dingy cap over a mop of brown curls, and rode away on his wheel [bicycle]."

Later, Netta arranged for Jack to be photographed for her article in his Klondike furs, and Charmian joined them for lunch afterward in a fashionable waterfront restaurant. This time Charmian was more captivated by the young man in the gray suit — especially his "wide-set, very large, direct eyes . . . as gray as the soft gray cloth, but more blue for the tan of his blond skin." She was impressed, as well, with "the beauty of his mouth, full-lipped, not small, with deep, upturned ends. . . ."

Charmian agreed at the lunch to review Jack's book *The Son of the Wolf*, which she had not yet seen. But when she did read the entire volume, she was so impressed by its raw power that she asked her aunt to be excused from the assignment. "I had no business," she wrote, "with the reviewing or criticizing of such brain-stuff as Jack London's." But Netta convinced her to re-consider, so she wrote the review.

Because Charmian was part of the literary world in the Bay Area, and because she was attractive, vi-brant, bright, and athletic, it was natural that she would soon begin attending Wednesday gatherings at the house of Jack London, the most popular new writer in California. Soon Jack and Charmian were finding every secret opportunity they could to be together. Their friends suspected nothing. Neither did Jack's wife, Bessie.

On July 14, 1903, after about a month of lies, Jack told Bessie that he was leaving her and the children. He would still pay for their support — he would make sure everyone was housed and clothed and fed — but he would no longer live with them. But the lies were not over. He did not tell her about Charmian. And Bessie still did not suspect her at all. In fact, she was positive that Jack was leaving her for Anna Strunsky. She accused Anna in the newspapers and said she

would never give Jack the divorce he wanted. She convinced a judge to issue a restraining order so Jack could
not have access to his bank accounts until their financial affairs were settled. When Jack agreed to build her
a house — and to pay her an allowance — the restraining order was lifted. He arranged for Macmillan to send
her a check for seventy-five dollars per month from his
earnings and agreed to pay for all her unusual expenses,
like medical bills.

Jack moved back to Oakland, where he lived a
while with Frank Atherton, his boyhood friend. Flora
and Johnny Miller came along, and would now live
nearby. But Jack and Charmian could not be together
in public. Not yet. This would have been a scandal that
would have ruined both of their reputations. Such
things simply were not done by respectable people in
the early 1900s. But they continued their discreet meetings.

Throughout the summer and fall of 1903, Jack
wrote passionate letters to Charmian, declaring his
love in long, sensuous sentences. "I have been wonder-
ing why I love you, and I think, in dim ways, that I
know I love you for your beautiful body, and for your
beautiful mind that goes with it. . . . You are more kin
to me than any woman I have ever known."

At first, Bessie was determined not to grant Jack a
divorce. She was bitterly angry and would not give him
what he most desperately wanted — his freedom. But
in August 1904, she decided she would file for divorce.
She charged Jack with desertion and cruelty. On Hal-

loween day there was a court hearing in Oakland. In mid-November the judge granted the divorce. Jack and Charmian now felt more confident and comfortable about being seen together in public. They had dinner in restaurants, went swimming and sailing, rode horses, attended plays, and looked at real estate. And Charmian, a superior stenographer and typist, began preparing Jack's manuscripts to send to publishers. It was a job she would do for the rest of his life.

EIGHT

1903–1916: By Land and by Sea

```
I hope, by May, to have a sloop on the
Bay and be writing a sea novel!
```
— Jack London, letter to Cloudesley Johns,
February 21, 1903

Jack London loved to travel. In his boyhood, the library books he read transported him to faraway, exotic lands. As a teenager he sailed on the San Francisco Bay, hunted seals in the Sea of Japan, and hopped trains across the continent. As a young man he shot the Whitehorse Rapids and floated down much of the length of the Yukon River.

Once his income began to grow, he was able to travel to places he had been able only to imagine as a child. When he received $750 from the *Saturday Evening Post* for *The Call of the Wild* early in 1903, he had a number of debts to clear up. His life had become more and more expensive, and he was spending money faster than he was making it. He was still supporting his mother and his nephew. Jennie Prentiss, his former nurse, needed money from time to time. She had never denied Jack; now he would not deny her. When Alonzo, her husband, died late in 1903, Jack brought her to his house in the Piedmont Hills and paid her to help take care of his daughters.

He was, of course, paying all expenses for Bessie and his daughters. And he would soon have yet another household to take care of — his and Charmian's. He was writing furiously every day to try to meet these expenses that seemed to inflate, balloonlike, with every breath of his success.

But once he had straightened out his finances, he decided to buy a sloop — a single-masted sailboat. He named his thirty-eight-foot vessel the *Spray* in honor of a boat owned by Joshua Slocum, an adventurer and writer. Slocum's book *Sailing Alone Around the World* (1900) had much impressed Jack. In the spring and summer of 1903 Jack took several small cruises on the *Spray* in the San Francisco Bay and up the rivers that empty into it. He continued, while aboard, to do his daily stint of writing.

At the time he was working on another novel, this one beginning with a young man aboard a San Francisco Bay ferryboat. One foggy morning he is washed overboard in a collision with another ferry. When he hits the water, he is stunned. "The water was cold — so cold that it was painful. . . . It was like the grip of death."

He is rescued by a seal-hunting vessel, the *Ghost*, on its way to the Sea of Japan. But to the young man's shock and anger, the captain will not turn back and put him ashore. One of his sailors has died unexpectedly. The ship needs another hand, and this wet young man will do. The captain's name is Wolf Larsen. The novel is *The Sea-Wolf*, one of Jack's greatest and most popular works.

By early 1904 Jack was so well known throughout the country that newspapers hired him from time to time to cover important events — from wars to boxing matches to public ceremonies. When a war broke out halfway around the world, the Hearst Newspaper Syndicate hired Jack to be a correspondent and photographer. Both Jack and Charmian were avid amateur photographers and took thousands of pictures of places and people all over the world.

This war was between Russia and Japan, ancient rivals for power in the Far East. At the time Jack sailed from San Francisco, war had not yet broken out. But everyone knew it was just a matter of time. The two sides could not agree about who should have influence in Korea. Japan had major investments in the country; Russia wanted to use Korea's harbors. Five months of negotiations had failed to bring a settlement, and so — without any warning — the Japanese Navy attacked the Russians in the Pacific Ocean.

In late January 1904 Jack arrived in Yokohama, Japan — a port he had visited as a teenager while hunting seals. The clouds of war were darkening ominously in the region. But lightning had not as yet struck. Jack did not have an easy trip across the ocean. He had caught the flu early in the voyage and had nearly broken his ankle in a shipboard accident. He spent three days in bed. He wrote to Charmian: "You should see me today. Quite the cripple, hobbling around on a pair of crutches. I can't stand on the ankle yet, but hope to be able to walk by the time we make Yokohama."

Within days of his landing, he was arrested by the Japanese police for taking unauthorized photographs. He spent a day in jail and had to go to court, where he was fined and had his camera taken away. It took America's minister in Tokyo to get it back for him.

Jack desperately wanted to get to where the fighting was expected to break out, but it required traveling in a land where he did not know the language. It was frustrating. "Hardest job I ever undertook," he wrote to Charmian. "Have had no news for several days, do not know if war has been declared. . . ."

Public transportation was very unreliable and controlled by the authorities. So Jack chartered private fishing boats to take him from place to place. He had some wild rides in the wintry ocean waters. "Never thought a sampan (an open crazy boat) could live through what ours did. A gale of wind, with driving snow — you can imagine how cold it was. . . . But we made it — half full of water — but we made it. . . . so cold that it froze the salt water."

At one small village, Jack was the first white man that the people had ever seen. He dazzled one old man by showing him his false teeth. The man could not believe his eyes — he shook Jack awake at three in the morning for one more look.

Eventually, he moved inland and now traveled by horseback, up to fifty miles a day. When he finally reached Pyongyang, Korea, he wrote to Charmian, complaining that he was "saddle-sore and raw" from his experience. Charmian, the expert rider, must have laughed aloud when she read it.

He was getting closer to the action. He saw movements of thousands of troops and heavy equipment. He was proud that he had gotten farther north than any other correspondent. But he was still forty miles from the fighting. And the physical discomforts were worsening. "Lice drive me clean crazy," he wrote. "I am itching all over."

In the middle of March, a disappointment: Jack was ordered back to Seoul, Korea, hundreds of miles to the south, away from the action. The authorities were not happy that he had moved north so quickly. For several weeks he was stuck in Seoul, frustrated, but still determined to reach the front.

Permission came to move ahead once again. By May 17 he had reached the headquarters of the Japanese Army across the Yalu River in the part of China known as Manchuria. But he still did not feel successful. He was being kept from the action. "I have so far done no decent work," he complained to Charmian. "Have lost enthusiasm and hardly hope to do any thing decent."

Disgusted, he was ready to leave for home when his quick fists landed him in trouble once again. Accompanying Jack along his journeys was a Korean cook and interpreter named Manyoungi. This young man told Jack that another servant was not letting him get enough of the feed for their horses. When Jack saw the

Japanese soldiers inspect Jack's credentials during his 1904 coverage of the Russo-Japanese War

person, he realized he was the same man who had stolen food on another occasion. Jack's temper flared, he swung, connected, and flattened the valet.

"Lord, Lord," he said to Charmian later, "I only hit him once — stopped him with my fist, rather — you know, he fell right into it; and then down with a thud. And he went around whimpering in bandages for two weeks."

Jack had made a serious mistake. His young victim was Japanese. Jack was immediately arrested and held for court-martial by the Japanese military authorities, who controlled the area. They didn't want Americans — even famous ones — striking their citizens. It took the intervention of U.S. President Theodore Roosevelt to free Jack from this one. A few days later he left the Far East aboard the SS *Korea*, bound for San Francisco.

Most of what we know about Jack London's experiences in Korea — and throughout the remainder of his life — is due to Charmian. Soon after her relationship with Jack began, she took control of much of his record-keeping. Although he had already been using ledgers to keep track of his sales to publishers, Charmian insisted that he save everything. In the past, when something had been published, Jack had usually just thrown away all the letters and manuscripts involved. This is why Jack's handwritten and typewritten copies of *The Call of the Wild* are gone. He simply discarded them.

Once Charmian took over these parts of his professional life, however, Jack's records become very accurate. His business letters, personal letters, manuscripts, notes for writing projects — most still exist. Charmian also kept a diary for most of her life. She did not usually write a lot each day, but she did write almost every day. Because of this, we know much of what Jack was doing most of the time for the last dozen years of his life.

Jack did not see his children very much as they were growing up. Although he was a dependable provider for them — he paid for their food, clothing, housing, and education — he was not an attentive father. His daughter Joan later wrote a book of memories about her father (*Jack London and His Daughters*) that was not published until 1990, nearly twenty years after she died. In the book, Joan remembered a number of

Jack's daughters, Becky (left) and Joan

happy times with "Daddy," but his visits were few, and the intervals between them lengthened. She recalled that she and her sister were "wildly happy" when he came to see them, but he never stayed long. He was, Joan wrote, "usually in such a hurry to keep appointments."

Just after New Year's, Jack decided to take another *Spray* cruise. This time it would be a working trip and would last for about two months. He took with him only his friend Cloudesley Johns and his valet, Manyoungi, who had returned from the Far East with him and would remain with him for about three years. Another friend went along, too — a new dog, Brown Wolf, a true husky from the Northland that had belonged to one of Jack's fellow gold rushers. Jack would one day write a story, "Brown Wolf," about a very similar dog that is forced to choose between his old and new masters.

On the *Spray* Jack worked on a new book, something he had only recently thought about. He had written to Brett in December that he would like to do what he called a "companion" to *The Call of the Wild*. But he wanted, he said, to "reverse the process." Instead of writing about a California dog that goes to the Yukon and returns to the wild, he would write about a wild Yukon wolf dog that becomes civilized and "retires" to California — to the same Santa Clara Valley where Buck had lived in the earlier novel. "It should make a hit," he wrote to Brett. "What d'ye think?" He had no idea, at first, for a title.

But when Brett finally wrote back saying Macmillan would be interested — just before Christmas 1904 — Jack replied: "I have figured on naming book after dog — *White Fang*, for instance, or something like that." He worked on the novel throughout most of 1905, finishing it on October 10. Like *The Call of the Wild* and *The Sea-Wolf*, it has remained one of Jack's most popular books. Several times it has been made into films.

Jack's story follows the life of White Fang, from his birth in the wild, to his capture by American Indians, his training as a sled dog, and his sale to the brutal "Beauty" Smith. Smith savagely beats the dog and teaches him to be vicious. Then he enters White Fang in life-and-death fights with other dogs — and even other animals. Men bet many hundreds of dollars on the outcome of these battles. White Fang always wins — until he faces a bulldog named Cherokee.

Once Jack finished writing *White Fang,* he was on the road within a week. He traveled by train again — this time, legally. He had become so popular that the Slayton Lyceum Bureau convinced him to take a nationwide lecture tour. He was already much in demand around the Bay Area, and officials at the Slayton Bureau believed that people all over the country would flock to hear this exciting new author. They were right.

On October 22, Jack gave his first speech on the tour to about five hundred people crowded into the high school gymnasium in Lawrence, Kansas. He did not look like a typical lecturer. Instead of a formal suit, he dressed a bit more casually in a soft, unstarched shirt and a white tie. He spoke clearly and with passion. He was an experienced speaker — he had learned a lot about "working a crowd" in the city parks of Baltimore and Oakland. And he had given many talks in the Bay Area. But many of the things he said while he was on tour were upsetting to some of the cultured and refined men and women who came to hear him in parts of the country that were more conservative and traditional than California.

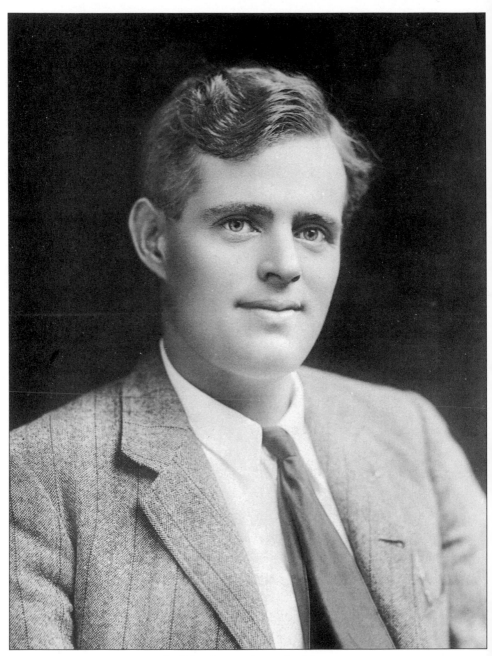

Jack London, author and celebrity

A Kansas City newspaper commented on his first speech — one of his fiery socialist talks called "Revolution." Although the topic was certainly controversial, the reporter mentioned that the audience enjoyed Jack's occasional humor. And, while telling in detail about the evils of child labor, he had apparently drawn tears from at least one woman in the audience. The reporter praised Jack's "great charm of manner" and observed that because he had "seen many great hardships," he had been able "to retain a sensitive sympathy for the troubles of other people."

On tour, Jack gave several different lectures. In the first month of the trip, it was usually "Revolution," his speech about the plight of the working class. He spoke at length about the poverty he had seen around the country. He listed statistics about the production of food and materials. He described sad conditions in factories. And he told stories about the suffering of individuals he had known.

He was most effective — as the woman in Kansas found out — while telling about child labor. "They never see the day," he said of child workers. "Those on the night shift are asleep when the sun pours its life and warmth over the world, while those on the day shift are at the machines before dawn and return to their miserable dens, called 'homes,' after dark. . . . Those who work on the night shift," he added, "are often kept awake by having cold water dashed in their faces." His speech usually ended with what he saw as the future: "Seven million men of the working-class say that they are going to get the rest of the working-class to join with them and take the management away. The revolution is here, now. Stop it who can."

But Jack spoke as well about more personal and less political subjects. He talked about the Klondike, his tramping days and time in prison, his struggles to become a writer, and his coverage of the Russo-Japanese War.

For the next month, Jack kept to a brutal schedule of travel and talking as he hopscotched his way across the Midwest and East. It was staggering. Charmian wrote later that "he swore he was getting enough train-travel to last all his life, and loathed it ever after."

On November 17, Jack received word that his divorce was final. He was free to marry Charmian, who was in Iowa visiting a friend and waiting to hear from him. He immediately telegraphed her to meet him in Chicago. On November 19, 1905, they were married at 10:00 PM by a justice of the peace. They spent one night in a Chicago hotel, and then Jack was back on tour, speaking the very next day in Lake Geneva, Wisconsin. He probably did not anticipate what a powerful reaction there would be to the announcement of his second marriage.

The lecture tour was in turmoil. Some newspapers were claiming — incorrectly — that Jack's new marriage was valid only in Illinois. Jack and Charmian knew this was ridiculous, but he issued a loud proclamation to the reporters who were now on the train with

Jack and Charmian early in their marriage

him: "If my marriage is not legal in Illinois, I shall re-
marry my wife in every state in the Union!"

Some of the women's clubs that Jack had been
scheduled to address now canceled his appearances. A
few libraries removed Jack's books from their shelves.
Newspapers criticized him. People were upset because
Jack had divorced, apparently abandoning his children,
and because he had married again so quickly. In the
early 1900s, such behavior was widely considered inde-
cent. He was not being a "good example." But as he
moved eastward, once more on tour, the criticism diminished a little.

In December Jack spoke in Massachusetts and

Maine, including two speeches at Harvard, the oldest
and most respected university in the United States. Jack
London, the ninth-grade graduate, speaking to one of
the most highly educated audiences in the country!
When he delivered "Revolution" to them, he got a reaction to one part of his speech that surprised and
angered him. While he was describing starvation in
Chicago, some of the students in the audience laughed.
They thought that he was exaggerating. Charmian,
who was in the audience that night, said that "Jack's
face [was] set like a vise," his eyes were flaming, and he
gave the students a tongue-lashing. She remembered
that "the response was instantaneous and whole-
hearted, the house rising as one man and echoing to
the applause until I, for one onlooker, choked and filled
with emotion. . . ."

At the end of December, Jack and Charmian left
for a brief honeymoon, sailing from Boston aboard the
Admiral Farragut. For about a week they toured Cuba
and Jamaica; then they sailed to Key West and Miami,
where they fished, saw the Everglades, and visited his-
toric sites. In mid-January, Jack returned to his tour in
New York City, where ten thousand people attended
his first lecture. Then it was on to New Haven, Con-
necticut, where Jack once again spoke to one of the
most educated audiences he would ever address, at Yale
University. Some newspapers were beginning to criticize Jack sharply for what he was saying — especially in
his "Revolution" speech. Editorials accused him of being anti-American, of lying about his statistics and

examples, of being wild and dangerous in his radical ideas, of encouraging revolution and violence. Some newspapers even condemned Yale and other places for giving Jack an opportunity to speak.

But Jack London never argued for the destruction of America, nor for the violent overthrow of the government. He was trying, the best way he could, to make people — especially rich and powerful and educated people — more aware of the problems faced by the working poor and the unemployed in the country. He felt that if Americans really understood how bad conditions were for the poor and for the workers, they would want to see major changes — the "revolution" he called for.

Jack was becoming exhausted. For months he had been on the road, crisscrossing the East and Midwest in trains that clattered and shuddered every inch of the way. He had been eating at banquets and in restaurants. He had been under constant pressure from the press about his marriage and about his socialist ideas. At times, audiences had greeted him only with hostility.

But at last Jack and Charmian began heading west. His last lecture stop was on February 3 in Grand Forks, North Dakota, where the crowd was so large the event had to be moved to a nearby armory. Following another appearance that evening before a capacity audience in the local opera house, he ended the tour. He was ready to go home. And on February 10, he was back in Oakland having dinner in a favorite restaurant with George Sterling and other close friends.

Jack and Charmian posing in an automobile

In most ways, Jack's one and only lecture tour was a success. Tens of thousands of people had seen him in person — all were now potential customers for his books. Also, by standing before crowds and defending his positions, he had been able to clarify what he really thought about a large range of subjects. It would help his future writing and speaking.

The Londons did not stay at home for long. They loved to travel, and for much of their marriage they visited places near and far. They journeyed by horseback, by wagon, by rail, by sailboat, by steamship — by just about every form of transportation available in the early 1900s. Although they never owned automobiles, they sometimes rode in ones belonging to others.

Their favorite activity, however, was sailing. In 1910 Jack bought another sailboat, the *Roamer*, a thirty-foot, two-masted vessel called a yawl. It replaced the *Spray*, the sloop he had sold a few years earlier. As with his earlier boats, Jack and Charmian spent a lot of time on board, sailing around the Bay and up into the Sacramento and San Joaquin rivers. He would complete his daily quota of writing in the mornings, then enjoy the

The Roamer, *Jack's 30-foot sailboat*

Hunting ducks aboard the Roamer

Reading at the wheel of the Roamer

rest of the day, occasionally fishing and duck-hunting from the deck.

Jack was excited about the *Roamer*. It was large enough to accommodate him and his friends, and it was maneuverable and quick enough to handle the unpredictable winds and tides. He wrote to a friend: "And I take my hat off to the old *Roamer*. I wouldn't trade her (for bay and river cruising) for any yacht I know or ever knew."

He took the boat out in October and November 1910, shortly after he bought it. In April 1911, Charmian and Jack were sailing for nearly another month on the inland waterways. Not all was smooth sailing on these trips. "At the present moment," he said in a letter, "we are lying high and dry on a mud flat . . . at the very southeasternmost end of San Francisco Bay. . . . I was sailing down the slough [marshy region] with a nice fair wind, when I missed the channel and went aground. . . ."

Between 1913 and 1915 Charmian and Jack took a few more trips aboard the *Roamer*. The last time was between September 1914 and January 1915, a cruise that lasted nearly five months. Not all of their time was spent aboard. Frequently they went ashore to meet friends, conduct business, go to the theater, visit doctors, go shopping, or eat in their favorite restaurant, the Saddle Rock in Oakland.

In the middle of January 1915, they left the *Roamer* for about a week and traveled up into the mountains near Truckee, California, for a "snow festival." Jack and Charmian got to ride in separate dogsleds. Charmian recalled later that "Jack's pleasure knew no bounds." He was back in an icy world he had loved as a young man, a world he had helped millions of his readers understand.

In 1911 Jack and Charmian took another unusual trip, this time by horse-drawn wagon through northern California and up into Oregon. They were gone nearly three months. Jack wrote that he and Charmian felt "it was about time we knew what we had in our own country and the neighboring ones." They did not want to take an automobile: "We don't mix with gasoline very well," he joked. And since Jack would have to do his daily writing and Charmian her daily typing, they could not travel by horseback. They would need to carry with them his writing supplies, some books, and the typewriter. They would also take along Nakata, a young Japanese valet who had come to work for them in 1907. Carrying so much required something substantial, so the Londons elected to use a light Studebaker trap, a type of wagon.

Jack had never driven a four-horse team. But he was fearless about trying new things. After a week-long

Jack, dressed in his Northland furs for a trip by sled near Truckee, California, in 1915

The Londons on their four-horse trip, near Fortuna, California

experiment with the animals, they set off in mid-June 1911. They did not camp out along the way, but tried to make sure they spent the night in hotels or in the homes of friends. Jack had some difficulty controlling the horses, which he humorously admitted. Charmian drove very little, writing later that "my strength was not quite equal to the weight of those long leathers in my hands for hours on end."

On the four-horse journey they tried a little bit of everything. They visited historical sites and great natural wonders, like Oregon's Crater Lake; canoed on the Klamath River with American Indians; fished and hunted; gathered wild strawberries; caught and ate eels; collected pretty stones on the ocean beaches; and drove through what Jack called "the most unthinkably glorious body of redwood timber to be seen anywhere in California." Jack paused in Medford, Oregon, to give a lecture. And in a saloon in Eureka, California, a volcanic discussion about socialism erupted into a fistfight.

Jack and Charmian embarked on yet another adventure — this one far more ambitious — in 1912. They decided that they would take a voyage aboard the freighter *Dirigo* from Baltimore to Seattle, via Cape Horn. Because the *Dirigo* was not a passenger ship, Jack, Charmian, and Nakata had to sign on as crew members: Jack was third mate, Charmian the stewardess, and Nakata an assistant steward. (The dog they took along, Possum, had no official title.) They knew the trip was a dangerous one; ships broken on the rocks would be visible from the deck. But they were confident in Captain Omar Chapman, a veteran of the voyage who was planning to retire when he reached Seattle.

The day before they were to sail, Jack came back to their Baltimore hotel with a surprise for Charmian: he had completely shaved his head — "naked as a billiard ball," Charmian complained. Jack snickered and laughed like a naughty child; Charmian cried for three hours. Later, she told him she thought she would trim a little of her own hair. She reached for the scissors and snipped away before the startled Jack. "But I only sheared off eight inches. I did not again look directly at Jack until there was at least half an inch of hair on his head."

When the Londons sailed, it was front-page news

in the *New York Times*. JACK LONDON SHIPS AS MATE, said the headline over the story; AND AUTHOR'S WIFE AS STEWARDESS ON 14,000-MILE VOYAGE was the subhead. "While Mr. London may be kept busy climbing the ship's ladders and washing decks, he takes with him his typewriters and a trunk full of paper for writing on his voyage."

It was a long and perilous trip. The *Dirigo* battled fierce winds, thick snow squalls, and high seas. For 148 days — nearly five months — they were at sea and saw land only once, Cape Horn itself. This sighting was unusual, for the area is frequently stormy and foggy. If it had not been for this very rare clear moment on the Horn, they would have seen no land at all. Jack described what they saw in *The Mutiny of the "Elsinore,"* a novel he wrote later about a similar voyage: "All of the land that was to be seen was snow. Long, low chains of peaks, snow-covered, arose out of the ocean. As we drew closer there were no signs of life. It was a sheer savage, bleak, forsaken land."

As usual, the Londons were working. For three hours each day Jack read aloud to Charmian from a variety of books. One of them was his old childhood favorite, *Signa*, which he had recently found in a used bookshop. Jack's writing project during the voyage was a novel, *The Valley of the Moon*, a story about a young married couple, Billy and Saxon Roberts, who decide to leave the city and travel on foot to look for property to farm. Not surprisingly, they travel through some of the same country the Londons had visited on their four-horse trip. Jack finished the novel aboard the ship. He also had notes for two other projects — *John Barley-corn*, the book about his continuing struggles with alcohol, and *The Mutiny of the "Elsinore."*

Charmian, without telling Jack, was working on some writing of her own, a short story called "The Wheel" about a ship whose crew fall asleep. When she showed it to Jack, he was encouraging. She eventually sold it to a magazine, though she never really thought it was much good.

Jack and Charmian delighted the crew of the *Dirigo* with their frequent boxing matches. They also climbed the masts for exercise. And Jack practiced a little dentistry, pulling teeth for members of the crew who were suffering. For one poor man, though, Jack probably should have declined to operate. He broke the tooth in half. They also tried to comfort Captain Chapman, who often complained of an upset stomach. They thought he might have food poisoning. But when they finally arrived in Seattle on July 26, 1912, they learned that Captain Chapman had cancer of the stomach. Two days later he died.

Because Jack was in demand as a journalist, he occasionally accepted assignments near his home in California, but he usually did not want to commit himself to more than a few days' work on any one project. But when *Collier's* magazine offered to pay him one thousand dollars per week — plus expenses — to report on an explosive political situation in Mexico, Jack readily

agreed. His debts were mounting, and this was a generous salary in 1914.

The United States had some oil fields in Tampico,
Mexico, on the Gulf Coast about two hundred miles
south of the Texas border. American sailors and soldiers were stationed nearby for security. One day, some
unarmed U.S. sailors in Tampico had strayed into a re-
stricted area; the Mexican authorities arrested and de-
tained them. The United States protested vigorously,
and the Mexican dictator, Victoriano Huerta, not
wanting to anger his huge neighbor to the north,
promptly released them with an apology. But the U.S.
authorities wanted more. They wanted the Mexican
military to punish the officer responsible and deliver a
twenty-one-gun salute to the American flag. Proudly
Huerta refused, and President Woodrow Wilson, seeing
an opportunity to weaken the dictatorship in the country, sent ships from the U.S. Navy to seize the harbor in
Vera Cruz, Mexico, about two hundred miles south of
Tampico. If the Americans controlled this harbor, the
Mexicans could not receive shipments of weapons
there. But the American move was costly: a firefight
broke out and continued for two days. Nineteen Americans and 126 Mexicans lost their lives.

Jack's assignment was to travel to Vera Cruz and
report on the situation. For much of the journey,
Charmian was with him. Jack was in the region for
about a month and filed about a half-dozen long stories
for *Collier's*. He visited U.S. warships, talked to officials

and soldiers, and also found time to go riding with Charmian, see bullfights, and go dancing, sightseeing, and shopping.

But he was not able to report any actual fighting — it was over before he arrived. As in Korea, however, he did a professional job of letting his readers know what it was like to be in Vera Cruz at a moment of extremely high tension. He told his readers, too, his opinion about war. "War is a silly thing," he wrote, "for a rational, civilized man to contemplate. To settle matters of right and justice by means of introducing into human bodies foreign substances that tear them to pieces is no less silly than ducking elderly ladies of eccentric behavior to find out whether or not they are witches."

Late in May, Jack began to feel queasy and realized he had the symptoms of bacillary dysentery, an intestinal disorder caused by contaminated food. Like all victims, he suffered from high fever, severe pain in the colon, and bloody diarrhea. In a letter he called it "a severe attack of rotten, bacillary, tropical dysentery." It was time to head for home.

Jack and Charmian loved California, but there was another place they learned to love nearly as much — Hawaii. At the end of February 1915, the Londons sailed for the islands aboard the *Matsonia*. For nearly five months they lived there, visiting friends, sailing, touring, attending concerts and dinners and parties, swimming on the beach at Waikiki, horseback riding . . . and, of course, working. Jack would write about ten pages each morning. He was working on two books, his first dog novels since *White Fang* nearly ten years before. They were called *Jerry of the Islands* and *Michael, Brother of Jerry*. Some people believe Jack wrote many animal stories, but of his fifty books, only four feature an animal as the main character.

The Londons returned to California in late July and five months later decided to return to Hawaii. They arrived three days before Christmas 1915, and once again began their rounds of tours, entertainments, and visits with friends. On several occasions they laughed themselves silly at the films of a popular new comedian, Charlie Chaplin.

But Jack was not feeling well. Injuries over the years to his knees and ankles had slowed him. Tropical diseases had weakened him. His kidneys were bothering him. Charmian reported that he did not swim or exercise much. He had trouble keeping down his breakfast. He would sleep away entire afternoons. Although he was not drinking heavily, he was drinking regularly after his day's stint of writing.

On July 26, 1916, they sailed for home. Jack would not visit Hawaii again. But he never forgot his affection for the place. In a long, three-part article called "My Hawaiian Aloha," Jack wrote about how much he loved the islands. "Come with your invitations, or letters of introduction, and you will find yourself immediately instated in the high seat of abundance. Or, come uninvited . . . and you will slowly settle into the Hawaiian heart. . . . You will have loved your way there, and you will find it the abode of love."

Jack's last visits to Hawaii were in 1915 and 1916; his first was in 1893 while seal-hunting aboard the *Sophia Sutherland*. In between was another visit — his first extended stay. And it occurred during perhaps the greatest adventure of his adventure-filled life.

NINE

1905–1909: The Cruise of the *Snark*

> Hawaii is the first port of call; and
> from there we shall wander through the
> South Seas, Samoa, Tasmania, New
> Zealand, Australia, New Guinea, and up
> through the Philippines to Japan. Then
> Korea and China, and on down to India,
> Red Sea, Mediterranean, Black Sea and
> Baltic, and on across the Atlantic to
> New York, and then around the Horn to
> San Francisco. . . . I shall not be in a
> rush; in fact, I calculate seven years
> at least will be taken up by the trip.
> — Jack London, letter to Bailey Millard, editor,
> *Cosmopolitan* magazine, February 18, 1906

In a long letter to *Cosmopolitan* magazine in 1906, Jack outlined the plans for a dream he and Charmian had been considering for some months. They would design and build their own yacht, load it with provisions, and sail it around the world at a leisurely pace, stopping where they wished for as long as they wished. They planned to explore waterways known and unknown and spend seven years or so living on a craft that sailed wherever their imaginations — and the wind — would take them. "If the whim strikes us," Jack wrote, "we'll go off to a thousand different and remote places that no tourist ever heard of."

The Snark *under construction*

Cosmopolitan, however, was not the only publication to receive the "dream" letter. Jack sent almost identical versions to other magazines and newspapers. He was looking for financing. He wanted a publisher to pay the way — in exchange for the exclusive rights to the articles he would write about their travels.

"It's going to cost me a lot of money to build this boat," he continued, "to outfit it, and to get instruments, charts, etc." He wanted a three-thousand-dollar advance. *Cosmopolitan* liked the idea and offered to advance him some of the money. Jack quickly accepted. "I'm going to turn out some crackerjack stuff on this trip!" he promised the editors of the magazine.

Jack and Charmian decided on a name for their vessel. It would be the *Snark*. Jack later claimed that they could not think of a better name, and so they selected this one from Lewis Carroll's humorous poem "The Hunting of the Snark." The poem tells about a mysterious creature that never is found by a bumbling, stumbling group of hunters. Friends suggested other names — *Sea Wolf* and even *Call of the Wild*. But Jack insisted there was no better name than *Snark*. They would spend about seven thousand dollars in construction and would sail from San Francisco Bay on October 1, 1906. Or so they planned.

The Londons wanted only the best for their yacht. It would be forty-five feet long. It would have four watertight compartments. There would be six feet of headroom below. There would be sails, but also a gasoline engine in times of emergency, or when the wind failed. It would have a launch and a separate lifeboat, as well. There would be a bathroom aboard — "a beautiful dream of schemes and devices, pumps, and levers, and sea-valves," wrote Jack. He spent a lot of time in the design of the bathroom. He probably laughed at himself if he remembered that Lewis Carroll had written that snarks have "five unmistakable marks" —

> *The fourth is its fondness for bathing-machines,*
> *Which it constantly carries about,*
> *And believes that they add to the beauty of scenes —*
> *A sentiment open to doubt.*

From the beginning, the building of the *Snark* was nearly a disaster. Jack later claimed that he dealt with forty-seven different unions and with 115 companies during the construction phase. He suffered delay after delay after delay. Materials were promised but delivered late or not at all. Materials were promised, and different, usually inferior, materials arrived.

Worst of all, the day the keel was to be laid, April 18, 1906, a major earthquake destroyed much of San Francisco. Trains that were going to bring materials for the building of the *Snark* were now needed to transport essential supplies for the tens of thousands of victims of the disaster. Carpenters who might have worked on ships were needed to rebuild homes and businesses.

San Francisco following the 1906 earthquake and fire

Within days of the earthquake, Jack was on the job, reporting the devastation for *Collier's* magazine. "San Francisco is gone," he told a shocked nation. "Nothing remains of it but memories and a fringe of dwelling houses on its outskirts. Its industrial section is wiped out. Its business section is wiped out. Its social and residential section is wiped out. The factories and warehouses, the great stores and newspaper buildings, the hotels and the palaces of the nabobs [rich people], all are gone. . . . Within an hour after the earthquake shock, the smoke of San Francisco's burning was a lurid tower visible a hundred miles away. And for three days and nights this lurid tower swayed in the sky, reddening the sun, darkening the day, and filling the land with smoke."

Jack went on to tell what he had seen as he wandered the streets of the burning city — the ridges and gaping holes in the streets, the destroyed lives, the personal side of the destruction. It was one of his most powerful pieces of reporting.

Somehow, work on the *Snark* began once again, but the Londons had to pay their workers nearly double the pre-quake wages. Jack and Charmian had appointed Roscoe Eames, husband of Charmian's Aunt Netta, to manage the construction of the *Snark* at Anderson's Ways in San Francisco. They could not spare the time. Jack was writing every day. Charmian was helping him. But they trusted Roscoe. He was a sailor, and he was family. But — as the Londons found out to their sorrow — he was an incompetent foreman. He

was careless, and inattentive to important details. Con-
tractors and carpenters used inferior materials right under his nose.

The date for sailing came and went. Days drifted
by. Weeks. Months. *Seasons*. The magazine publishers
were alarmed. They had advanced Jack thousands of
dollars. He was supposed to sail and write his stories
and articles. But the *Snark* was still sitting in drydock,
under construction. By November, fourteen men were
working on the vessel. Costs were soaring. By January,
Jack had spent more than $15,000 on his $7,000 dream.

On February 10, 1907, more than four months beyond their original deadline, they launched the *Snark*
for a ten-mile trial run out to sea. The boat leaked. The
engine wouldn't work properly. Later, tied up at a dock,
it was nearly crushed between two barges. During its
final overhauling, the *Snark* was stuck in the mud. It
took two tugboats to pull it free.

Jack was frustrated. The *Snark* had now cost him
nearly $30,000. But he was not going to give up. He
would sail to Hawaii, no matter what. On April 16 the
unfinished boat was towed to a wharf in Oakland. For
two days they loaded their supplies — including a
phonograph and five hundred records! And then a U.S.
Marshal appeared; the *Snark* could not sail until Jack
paid a debt of $232. His creditors were afraid he would
die at sea, and they would never be paid.

Finally, on April 23, the *Snark* was underway. Jack
had said good-bye to his daughters, Joan and Becky, the
night before. He promised to write to them and to bring

The Snark

them gifts, but Joan later wrote about the anguish she and her sister felt that night. *A trip of seven years!* She was "pierced," she said, "by the realization that now Daddy was really going away from us for so long that it might as well be forever."

The dock was crowded with reporters and friends of the Londons; many were sure they would never see Jack and Charmian again. As the *Snark* sailed through the Golden Gate, she was leaking just about everywhere. Seawater soaked and ruined food. Nothing worked. Some of the hands were seasick, vomiting over the side. The boat did not maneuver properly into the wind. But they were headed for Hawaii, more than two thousand miles away.

Jack and Charmian were not alone on the *Snark*. They brought along Roscoe Eames, who served as navigator but who proved to know as little of navigation as he did about supervising a construction crew. Martin Johnson, a young man from Independence, Kansas, had written to Jack to ask for a job on the yacht — just as many, many other people had done when word of the voyage had reached the public. Think of it . . . seven years on the high seas in company with Jack and Charmian London, two of the most interesting people of the day! Four days after Martin wrote to Jack, he received a telegram. He later remembered the moment in a book of his own, *Through the South Seas with Jack London*:

"'Can you cook?' it asked.

'Sure, try me,' I replied."

He immediately ran out to a friend who worked in a restaurant. Martin Johnson needed cooking lessons. When he arrived in Oakland, Martin lived with the Londons for three months while the boat was readied. He learned more about cooking — this time from Jennie Prentiss, who, Martin wrote, told "me things that no cook-book in the world could have told me."

The Londons also brought along Paul Murakami, called Tochigi, their Japanese valet. A young Stanford University student, Herbert Stoltz, would be engineer. Jack and Charmian had cabins below in the bow of the *Snark*; Roscoe had a cabin near the engine room (toward the stern); the others slept in the main cabin or on deck in hot weather.

"It was a beautiful, bright, sunshiny day when we passed out of the Golden Gate," Martin Johnson wrote, "with hundreds of whistles tooting at us a farewell salute, passed the Seal Rocks, and turned . . . westward."

There were serious problems. The crew members discovered the first day that Roscoe did not know how to navigate in the open ocean. He was an experienced inland sailor, but had never tried to find his way at sea. But Jack was ever confident in his ability to teach himself anything and had brought along books about navigation. He would learn to navigate by navigating. And the day he finally figured out what he was doing, he said he "felt the thrill and tickle of pride. . . . I was a worker of miracles . . . I had listened to the voices of the stars and been told my place upon the highway of the sea."

He must have learned well, because on May 17 they sighted land, and on May 20 they arrived in the Hawaiian Islands. "In the early morning we drifted around Diamond Head into full view of Honolulu," Jack wrote; "and then the ocean burst suddenly into life. Flying fish cleaved the air in glittering squadrons." They had been at sea twenty-seven days. Customs officials tossed them a newspaper that announced that the *Snark* and all on board had been lost at sea.

The Londons were in Hawaii for five months. The *Snark* needed extensive repairs, and some crew members needed to be replaced. Tochigi's stomach refused to accept food while he was on a boat, and the Londons were completely fed up with Roscoe. In a letter to Netta, Jack exploded, criticizing her husband's "colossal incompetence . . . no more a seaman than I am an Egyptian dancing-girl." Herbert Stoltz left the cruise, as well, to continue his studies at Stanford.

Jack tried to find replacements. He ended up firing some people he had hired before the yacht ever went back to sea. Hiring and firing — including a captain who was a paroled murderer — went on throughout the voyage.

While they were in Hawaii, they made many friends — friends they would return to see in 1915. They toured the islands, visited volcanoes, hunted, fished, and swam. Jack found time for a fistfight in a saloon. He even tried a sport that was popular on the Hawaiian beaches — surfing.

Jack London is one of the reasons that surfing is now a popular sport. In October 1907, he published an article in *Woman's Home Companion* called "Riding the South Sea Surf." Surfing, said Jack, was "a royal sport for the natural kings of earth." He was exhilarated when he saw his first surfers: "And suddenly out there where a big smoker [wave] lifts skyward, rising like a sea god from out of the welter of spume and churning white, on the giddy, toppling, overhanging and downfalling, precarious crest appears the dark head of a man. . . . His heels are winged, and in them is the swiftness of the sea. In truth, from out of the sea he has leaped upon the back of the sea, and he is riding the sea that roars and bellows and cannot shake him from his back."

He had to try it himself. In the article, he told about his first attempts and described the actual process of surfing — or "surf-riding," as he called it. He was not immediately successful. He paddled on his board out a ways. But struggle as he might, he could not stand and ride. "I tried for a solid hour, and not one wave could I persuade to boost me shoreward." Finally, another surfer showed him the problem — his board was too short.

On one of his first trips to the shore, he stood too far forward on his new board and "was tossed through the air like a chip and buried ignominiously under the downfalling breaker."

Finally, he learned the tricks of riding and the next day spent four glorious hours surfing. He could not

Surfing in Hawaii (Jack is kneeling on his board)

wait for the next day. But it did not come — not for a while. Jack had a horrible sunburn, so bad he could not walk. His eyes were nearly swollen shut. He confessed that he was writing the surf-riding article in bed.

During one of their tours in Hawaii, Jack and Charmian visited Molokai, an island home to people who suffered from leprosy. At this time in history, people were terrified of the disease. It does, indeed, have a frightening course for many who have it. It attacks the skin, nerves, and muscles. Although the disease is contagious, it is not highly so. And it is not usually fatal, although sufferers can be weakened by it and die of other diseases. The progress of leprosy can be slowed, but not cured, and its damage cannot be reversed.

Jack and Charmian were fearless explorers. They rode horses into the craters of volcanoes, sailed the ocean in a leaking boat, and tried just about everything they could in life. But many people thought they were crazy when they decided to visit with the lepers on Molokai. "We mingled freely with them," wrote Jack, "and before we left, knew scores of them by sight and name. . . . the awful horror with which the leper has been regarded in the past, and the frightful treatment he has received have been unnecessary and cruel."

The Londons saw things both wonderful and horrible. They joined the lepers on the Fourth of July in horseback riding and shooting, and in the evening attended a songfest and dance. Jack pleaded in his own writing for more understanding, more sympathy, and more money for research on the disease. "Not for their sakes merely, but for the sake of future generations, a few thousands of dollars would go far. . . ."

While at sea, and while in Hawaii, Jack continued his daily writing routine — Martin Johnson recalled that Jack wrote for two hours every day. During this time he created what is perhaps his best-known short story, "To Build a Fire." He also wrote an article, "Adventure," which eventually became Chapter 2 of his book about the voyage, *The Cruise of the "Snark"* (1911), and he began writing some of his many short stories set in the islands. Charmian was productive, as well, continuing to write in her diary and keeping notes for her own book of the voyage, *The Log of the "Snark"* (1915). In August Jack started writing one of his greatest novels, *Martin Eden*, the story of a young man who struggles up from poverty and ignorance to become a successful writer.

When the repairs to the *Snark* were finally completed, they took a trial run on October 6, then set sail the following day for the Marquesas Islands, two thouand miles south and a little east of Hawaii. It would take them two months.

After about a month at sea, they discovered that a faucet on one of their freshwater tanks had accidentally been left on and they had a mere ten gallons left, enough for only 20 days. They now had to ration water in one of the hottest climates on earth. "Our thirst grew almost unbearable," wrote Martin Johnson. "We spoke of nothing but water. We dreamed of water." Finally, a thunderstorm struck the *Snark*, and they were able to spread out canvas and collect water enough to refill their tanks.

On November 30, they crossed the equator, reaching land on December 6. The Marquesas Islands were far more primitive than Hawaii, but they still managed to make friends and to spend time exploring. They sailed on to Tahiti, another one thousand miles or so to the southwest. This island had regular steamship service, so the Londons collected much of the mail they had been expecting. But they received bad news. Netta Eames, who had been in charge of the Londons' financial affairs back in Oakland, had proved nearly as incompetent as Roscoe Eames had been at sea.

They would have to leave the *Snark* in Tahiti for about a month and return to California. They sailed aboard the steamship *Mariposa* on January 13, 1908. About two weeks later, they were having dinner with George Sterling at the Saddle Rock restaurant in Oakland and answering the countless questions of inquiring reporters. For a week they remained in California, straightened out their finances, visited Jack's daughters, and sailed once again for Tahiti on February 2. Shortly after his return, Jack finished *Martin Eden*.

From Tahiti, the Londons sailed through the Society Islands, to Bora Bora — and then another twelve hundred miles west to Samoa. Here they saw one of the most thrilling sights of their lives — an active volcano. They had trouble approaching the erupting island in

Jack and Charmian aboard the Snark

the *Snark*, for lava was pouring into the water, steam was swirling around them, hot cinders scorched their clothes, and fiery winds blew in their faces.

Once safely ashore, they visited the charred remains of homes and villages. They poked sticks into rivers of lava, watching them immediately transform into torches. They stuck coins into molten lava, coating them for souvenirs. They marveled at what the volcano had spared — a small graveyard. Just outside it, the flow had for some reason separated, missing the cemetery entirely.

From Samoa, they sailed southwest to the Fiji

Islands and the New Hebrides and north to the Sol-
omon Islands, which lie over a thousand miles north-
east of Australia. At virtually every island, they were
greeted by the residents and government officials with
great ceremony. They were taken on guided tours and
wined and dined. They gathered huge collections of
masks and weapons and works of art from the island
people.

But just about everyone aboard was sick. Jack
had malaria and severe problems with his digestion.
Both Jack and Charmian suffered from yaws — open,
raspberry-colored sores on their bodies. One on Jack's
foot was so bad that he feared he would need amputa-
tion. The yaws seemed to respond to no medicine the
Londons tried. Jack's hands were swelling and peeling
in alarming fashion. As the summer of 1908 became
fall, Charmian worried that Jack would die at sea. But
still he wrote every day. "The *Snark* has been a hospital
for months," he wrote, "and I confess that we are getting used to it."

Alarmed by Jack's deteriorating health, the Londons temporarily left the *Snark* and sailed south on another ship to Sydney, Australia. A doctor told Jack he
did not have leprosy — a fear, because of Molokai. But
he stayed in the hospital for five weeks. He was suffering terribly. "I was as helpless as a child," he wrote. "On
occasion my hands were twice their natural size, with
seven dead and dying skins peeling off at the same
time. There were times when my toenails, in twenty-
four hours, grew as thick as they were long."

The Londons knew they could not go on. Jack could not help out on the yacht and he would be useless in an emergency. They would have to sell the *Snark*, return to California, and hope that he would heal.

Once the crew brought the *Snark* to Australia, they dispersed. Martin Johnson continued on around the world on a steamship. The others worked their ways home. In early April, Jack and Charmian and their valet, Nakata, boarded the *Tymeric*, a steamship loaded with coal, bound for Ecuador. Jack's hands must have improved along the way, for he challenged officers on the ship to boxing matches. He wrote to his friend George Sterling that he had blackened the eye of one, puffed the face of another, and doubled the size of the nose of a third. He admitted that his own face had a number of discolorations and that he developed cramps in his legs — "but I'm getting into condition," he said. "Haven't had a drink for a month."

Jack's boxing may have been inspired by an event he had seen and written about in Sydney — a championship boxing match featuring one of the most famous heavyweight boxers in history, Jack Johnson. Johnson was an African American and, in a time of ferocious racial prejudice against his people, he was fighting a white man, Tommy Burns. Just about everyone in the crowd — including Jack — was rooting for Johnson to lose.

Johnson thoroughly defeated Burns — knocking him out in the fourteenth round after bashing him around at will. Jack wrote about the event fairly. "Because a white man wishes a white man to win," he wrote, "this should not prevent him from giving absolute credit to the best man who did win, even when that best man was black. All hail to Johnson." Jack accurately reported that Johnson toyed with Burns — talking to him and smiling throughout the fight. He was very impressed with Jack Johnson, one of the greatest athletes of the day.

They arrived in Ecuador in mid-May, and after about a month sailed for Panama, then to New Orleans, where they were swarmed over by reporters. In mid-July they were on a train for home.

The mysterious swelling in Jack's hands gradually disappeared after he left the tropics, but the diseases of that region had weakened him severely. He would never again be the vigorous young man who could shovel coal for twelve hours or captain his own yacht around the world. He would sail occasionally on the *Roamer* on the inland waterways he loved, but in the future his ocean voyages were aboard the ships of others.

And the *Snark?* It sold for three thousand dollars — about one-tenth of what Jack had paid for it. The last anyone saw of it, it was a near-wreck and apparently abandoned in the New Hebrides Islands.

TEN

1905–1916: Sailor on Horseback

> For a long time I have been keeping
> steadily the idea in mind of settling
> down somewhere in the country.
> — Jack London, letter to George Brett, May 26, 1905

Even before Jack and Charmian were married, they were in love not only with each other but with a beautiful valley only about fifty miles north of San Francisco — the Sonoma Valley, also known by the American Indians as the Valley of the Moon.

Jack first saw the area in May 1903, just before his marriage with Bessie dissolved. In the little town of Glen Ellen, Charmian's aunt, Netta Eames, owned a summer home called Wake Robin Lodge, named for the lovely, lilylike plants with white blossoms that grow thickly in the area and bloom in early spring, before the robins return.

On the property were several guest cabins where Jack and his family stayed. But Jack did not linger there long; he returned to work on his writing at his home in the Piedmont Hills, where he would be uninterrupted by children and family responsibilities.

When he returned from covering the Russo-Japanese War in 1905, Jack once again stayed at Wake Robin Lodge as the guest of Charmian and her aunt. He was very depressed at the time. His experiences in

Korea had frustrated him; his divorce was dragging along in the courts; a flood of financial responsibilities threatened to overwhelm him. Charmian, sensing his mood, invited him to walk with her along Graham Creek, but, she wrote, "to my hidden sorrow, he appeared to have grown blind to the beauty he had so loved." Charmian asked him if the loveliness in the world meant nothing to him anymore.

"I don't seem to care for anything — I'm sick, my dear," he replied. It was what he called the Long Sickness — a deep depression that brought him very near to total despair.

The day Jack was to leave Glen Ellen, Charmian suggested they ride a different way, through the redwood-lined Nunn's Canyon. She was certain Jack was slipping away from her and perhaps from life itself. But the scenery began, somehow, to work on his mood. "The morning," Charmian wrote later, "was one of California's most blessed, a great broken blue-and-white sky. . . . As we forged skyward on the ancient road, . . . I could see my dear man quicken and sparkle as if in spite of himself and the powers of darkness."

The Long Sickness was lifting, right before her eyes. Suddenly, he was once again talking enthusiastically about the future. He would move into one of the Wake Robin cabins with Manyoungi, his valet at the time. She did not understand at first what had happened — it was "some sweet miracle," she said, and "one of the supreme moments of my life."

Jack lived at Wake Robin in the spring of 1905

and spent many happy hours riding through the canyons, the magnificent stands of towering redwoods, across crystal streams and mountain pastures. He decided that he wanted to live in the Glen Ellen area permanently. He and Charmian began looking at real estate.

Early in June they rode to examine a parcel of land called the Hill Ranch. The moment Jack saw the 130-acre property he knew he had to own it. He quickly agreed to the $7,000 price, made a $500 down payment, and promptly wrote to Brett at Macmillan asking for a $10,000 advance. Within two weeks he had hired a ranch foreman, bought some livestock and equipment, made plans for a new barn, and broken ground for it. His letters during the time show his boundless enthusiasm for his new project. He wrote to Brett:

> There are great redwoods on it, some of
> them thousands of years old — in fact,
> the redwoods are as fine and magnificent
> as any to be found anywhere outside the
> tourist groves. Also there are great
> firs, tan-bark oaks, maples, live-oaks,
> white-oaks, black-oaks, mandrono and man-
> zanita galore. There are canyons, sev-
> eral streams of water, many springs,
> etc., etc. . . . All I can say is this — I
> have been over California off and on all
> my life, for the last two months I have
> been riding all over these hills, look-
> ing for just such a place, and I must say
> that I have never seen anything like it.

Jack seated on a bench carved from the trunk of a redwood

On the property there was no place where they could immediately live, so following their marriage in November 1905, the Londons moved into the main house at Wake Robin in Glen Ellen. "Oh, take my word," he wrote to his old friend Frederick Irons Bamford, "there is no place like the country."

A few months later, in February 1906, Jack bought a home in Oakland for his mother, nephew, and Jennie Prentiss. Upstairs was a large room reserved for Jack and Charmian whenever they were in the city — a sort of townhouse for them. Flora lived there for the rest of her life. Jack and Charmian would never again live anywhere else but Glen Ellen.

While they were away on the *Snark* cruise, the Londons left their business affairs in the hands of Netta Eames, who made a number of unwise and even unethical decisions about the Londons' money. Mixed in among her misjudgments, however, were a few shrewd decisions. For ten thousand dollars she acquired the La Motte Ranch, a 127-acre property not far from Jack's original purchase. In one stroke, she had nearly doubled his holdings. Then she proceeded to buy the Kohler and Fish ranches, another thirty-three acres. The last three purchases, however, were not connected to his first one. In between was a fingerlike section of a huge seven-hundred-acre property, part of which contained a winery.

When the Londons returned from the *Snark* cruise, they continued to plan projects for the property — Jack would call it "Beauty Ranch" — and they resumed buying livestock and equipment for the vast enterprise they were dreaming about. In May 1910, the neighboring acreage became available, and for $26,000 Jack once again more than doubled his holdings in Glen Ellen. He now owned nearly eleven hundred acres, but not the portion where the winery buildings stood. That purchase of an additional twelve acres occurred almost exactly a year later. And a year and a half afterward, he bought the final piece he would own — the four-hundred-acre Freund Ranch. He had made seven purchases; all were now connected into one fourteen-hundred-acre working ranch.

When Jack and Charmian returned from their

Jack surveying his beloved Valley of the Moon

four-horse trip to Oregon in September 1911, they slept for the first time in a cottage that had been part of the old winery property. Since 1910 Eliza Shepard, Jack's stepsister, had lived on the ranch and had assumed the duties of ranch superintendent. While the Londons were away, she had prepared the cottage for their return. It was comfortable, but small. Jack did not intend to live there long; he had already begun plans for yet another spectacular project — the building of his "dream house" on a hillside overlooking the entire Valley of the Moon. He called it "Wolf House."

Wolf House would be spacious and many-roomed, but not a mansion — not in the normal sense of that word. Jack and Charmian designed their home to accommodate their many interests, their work, and their

Architect's drawing for Wolf House

collections from the South Seas and elsewhere. Charmian called it "a big cabin, a lofty lodge, a hospitable tepee. . . ." The Londons tried to use local materials as much as possible in the construction of Wolf House. The exterior walls were stone, dragged up to the site by horse from a quarry across the valley; the supports and frame were redwood; the roof, red Spanish tile.

Wolf House was U-shaped, about eighty-six feet wide, each leg of the U about eighty-two feet long. It was a four-level structure. The lowest level — below the ground level — was basically the maintenance section. It held the kitchen, the dining room, storage, servants' quarters, and a large "stag party room."

Dominating the second level were a reflection pool —
which the Londons decided to adapt for a swimming
pool as well — and a large library, now needed to hold
Jack's thousands of volumes. The level also featured a
two-story living room, three guest suites, a gun and tro-
phy room, and space for Charmian's grand piano. The
third level had what they called an "arcade" — a bal-
cony and walkway that overlooked the reflecting pool.
It was also the "writing level" of the house: Jack's "work
den" was on one end, Charmian's area on the other.
Jack's den had a stairway directly down to the library,
and Charmian's room opened onto a sun deck. On the
fourth level — really the roof — was Jack's "sleeping
tower," open to the air. Another tower held water di-
verted from a nearby stream; Wolf House would have
natural running water.

Construction took nearly two years. By the time
the house was ready, Jack estimated he had spent forty
thousand dollars. The only insurance he held on it was
a six-thousand-dollar policy for protection during the
construction phase. On August 22, 1913, the house was
just about ready for occupation. Workmen had been
finishing some of the woodwork and floors with linseed
oil. The Londons would soon begin moving in.

But around midnight that night, Charmian was
awakened by the sounds of voices outside. "Tiptoeing
out," she wrote, "I saw Eliza, by his bedside, point in the
direction of the Wolf House half a mile away, where
flames and smoke rose straight into the windless, star-
drifted sky." Wolf House had erupted in flames. By the

Wolf House, nearing completion

time the blaze was discovered, it was too late. The fire sought out and consumed every piece of wood in the structure — the supports, the floors, the rafters, the bookshelves. When the fire was eventually extinguished, the interior had collapsed, and nothing remained but some crumbling stone walls. It was gone, all gone.

Jack several times wrote to people about his plans to rebuild. But he never did. It would require another enormous investment of money, and his income was already stretched to the limit.

Both Jack and Charmian London went to their graves without knowing for certain what had caused the Wolf House fire. In the spring of 1995 — more than eighty years after the fire — a team of forensic investigators studied the site and the walls (some are still standing) and determined the cause. The fire had broken out in the dining room, where some rags soaked in linseed oil had been carelessly left that night. They had ignited by spontaneous combustion. The fire exploded up the nearby staircase, which acted like a chimney. All the fresh air that Jack had wanted in the house now acted like the breath from a giant bellows, fanning the flames into an inferno that destroyed the building.

But the ranch remained. The cottage remained. There was work to be done, and Jack threw himself into his many, many other projects. And in his work, he found peace. Between his first ranch purchase in 1905 and his death in 1916, Jack made enormous improvements in his properties. He attacked ranching the way he attacked everything else he wanted to know about: he read every book, magazine, and pamphlet he could find on the subject. So it was he learned about virtually every aspect of the country life. He wrote proudly to Brett late in 1914: "I am building, constructing, and making the dead soil live again."

He constructed and repaired buildings. He bought a blacksmith shop in Glen Ellen and had all the equipment hauled to the ranch. He planted and harvested hay. He studied farming techniques of the ancient Chinese — especially concerning plowing and drainage — and borrowed freely from every source that seemed to work. He applied no artificial fertilizers but used the manure of his own animals. He grew spineless cactus to feed his cattle. He rotated crops so as not to exhaust the soil. He wired buildings for electricity. He built the first concrete-block silos in California — forty feet tall — and filled them with feed. From England he imported the famous shire horses and began to breed them. One of his animals — named Neuadd Hillside — took first prize at the California State Fair.

In 1915 he designed and built what many considered a foolish facility: a "pig palace." In the center of the palace was a small tower holding the food, and surrounding it were nineteen individual "apartments" for

Jack in his "pig palace" on Beauty Ranch

each sow. Water could flow, when needed, to the entire structure. The pigs' manure was piped to a storage tank elsewhere on the ranch to be used as fertilizer. The palace cost three thousand dollars, but Jack estimated it would soon pay for itself because of all the time and energy he would save in the care and feeding of his animals.

About a mile up the hillside from the cottage, Jack's workers built a stone dam across a stream, forming a lake that was used for both recreation and irrigation. It covered five acres and held seven million gallons. He also built a redwood bathhouse on the site, which quickly became a favorite spot for the Londons and their guests on hot afternoons.

The Londons expanded and remodeled the cottage and the nearby carriage house, which was used for guests. They added a den to the cottage to store just a few of the books in Jack's eighteen-thousand-volume library. An adjacent building — once part of the wine-making system — was divided into segments and became their kitchen, dining, and laundry rooms. On the front of the cottage were two small sleeping porches, one for Jack, one for Charmian. They did not sleep together: Jack worked late into the night, and Charmian suffered from insomnia.

In the cottage on the ranch, the Londons kept a brisk routine of working and entertaining. As usual, Jack would produce his daily thousand to fifteen hundred words in the morning. Charmian would type them. They would not usually join their guests until lunch — and there seemed always to be guests. In the afternoons, they would ride around the ranch, swim, and otherwise enjoy the California climate. After supper, there would be games with the guests or music on the phonograph. Or Jack would read aloud from his latest work. Then he would carry off to his room boxes of books and other materials for his long night's work. He slept only a handful of hours each night.

It was while living such a life that Jack completed the last two novels he would live to see published. First was *The Star Rover* (1915). It is a strange story that Jack based on the experiences of an ex-convict from San Quentin named Ed Morrell (1869?–1938?). While Morrell was in prison, he had been tortured cruelly, and he claimed that he had escaped the agony through the process of "astral projection." During the torture sessions, he was able, he said, to cause his spirit to leave his body. His spirit was then able to travel across time and space. He became a "star rover." Jack had heard about Morrell and invited him to the ranch in November 1911. He stayed nearly a month and told the Londons about his prison experiences. Jack believed that Morrell's story would make a fascinating novel. He took notes and began writing in 1913.

The final novel Jack lived to see published, *The Little Lady of the Big House* (1916), is a story interesting now only because the main characters so much resemble Jack and Charmian. They are named Dick and Paula Forrest. They live in a place like Wolf House on a ranch near Glen Ellen, which the Forrests have made a center for writers and artists and philosophers of all sorts. Dick is a writer of books about ranching. Paula is a beautiful, talented woman with strong opinions and a frank manner.

Jack's dream was that the ranch would become a totally self-sufficient community. They would grow their food. On the property would be living quarters for his workers, even a store, perhaps a school for the children. It would become a center for writers and artists. And, for a while — a short while — much of this happened.

ELEVEN

1916: Final Days, Final Hours

And I, dying, will remember sweet Charmian.
— Jack London, letter to Charmian Kittredge,
October 20, 1903

In his forty-first year, 1916, Jack London was not well. The tropical diseases from the *Snark* voyage had, in some ways, permanently disabled him. He walked only painfully because of a series of accidents over the years to his knees and ankles, and because of rheumatism. His gums were sore and occasionally bled. The dysentery he had contracted in Mexico had hurt him deeply. His heart and lungs had been damaged by a quarter-century of heavy smoking. Charmian recalled that since he was fourteen, Jack "had smoked all his waking hours — in the daytime, at work, or at play, at night when reading or studying. . . ." His kidneys, weakened by illness and by bouts with alcohol, were painful and unreliable. He had not been drinking heavily in recent years, but the damage had been done. He was often in pain, and slept even less than usual.

He had sustained psychological shocks, as well: the interruption of the *Snark* cruise, the fire at Wolf House, the death of friends. Mabel Applegarth, the first woman he loved, had died of tuberculosis in February 1915. He had kept in touch with her over the years, had watched her weaken and die.

He was depressed about growing older. "My lean runner's stomach has passed into the limbo of memory," he wrote. "The joints of the legs that bear me up are not so adequate as they once were. . . . Never again can I run with the sled-dogs along the endless miles of Arctic trail." He realized that "under that rind of flesh which is called my face is a bony, noseless death's head." He was aware that he was dying.

He was not getting along well with his teenage daughters. They had grown up in their mother's house in Oakland, and Jack did not see them often. He felt Bessie had turned his daughters against him — indeed, she never allowed Becky and Joan to visit their father at the ranch. There were many misunderstandings, and unkind letters went back and forth.

He was under constant pressure to produce. The enormous expenses from the *Snark*, from Wolf House, and from the ranch operation were draining him. He once estimated his monthly payroll was fifteen hundred dollars. He was supporting Flora and Johnny Miller, Bessie, his daughters, and Jennie Prentiss. He was generous with friends, too, often loaning money that he never saw again. He had made some bad investments and was constantly struggling with the new motion picture industry about the rights to film his stories.

In 1913 he even expressed a weariness with writing. To a young writer who had asked for advice, Jack snapped: "I do not like to write for a living . . . if I had my way I should not write a single line . . . I am so tired of writing that I'd cut off my fingers and toes in order to avoid writing." It wasn't that he hated the acts of imagining and creating — he had simply tired of the never-ending pressure to *produce*. He spent money before he got it, then had to write in order to earn it. It was a nasty cycle, and his letters during his final years are full of pleas to publishers for advances, of promises to produce, produce, produce.

There were other nagging concerns, as well. From time to time people claiming to be Jack London would write bad checks or otherwise misrepresent him. Numerous times he had to straighten out misunderstandings caused by this plague of "doubles."

On other occasions he was accused of plagiarism. Jack sometimes borrowed ideas from books, magazines, and newspapers he read. When he was writing *The Call of the Wild*, for example, he used information from a true story he had recently read, *My Dogs in the Northland*, by Egerton R. Young. From Young's book Jack took names of dogs and even some incidents. But he argued that borrowing ideas from Young's book, a true story, was no more wrong than using information from an encyclopedia or other reference book or using something someone had told him about. Jack was never formally sued for plagiarism. But the accusations bothered him.

He had a falling-out with the socialists, too. In March 1916 both Jack and Charmian abruptly resigned from the Socialist Party. He said in his letter that his resignation was due to the party's "lack of fire and fight, and its loss of emphasis on the class struggle."

There were other events that had hurt Jack. On

June 19, 1910, Charmian gave birth to a daughter who
lived only thirty-eight hours. In March 1912, Charmian
was once again pregnant. But in August, a month after
they returned from their *Dirigo* voyage around Cape
Horn, she miscarried. Jennie Prentiss was there, trying
to help. "A second blighting disappointment," wrote
Charmian. And Jack, she added, "was sadly cast down,
though he said little."

November 1916 was a busy and frustrating month
for Jack. A lawsuit involving water rights on his property forced him to spend several days on the witness
stand. Friends arrived at the ranch for visits. He was

At Beauty Ranch, November 1916

struggling hard to do his daily writing. On November 16, a newsreel company came to the ranch and took the only known motion pictures of Jack. He showed the pig palace and cuddled a piglet for the camera. He looked tired, overweight — older than his forty years.

On Tuesday, November 21, he wrote a letter to his daughter Joan — his last letter to anyone. The tone was much friendlier than in earlier letters. He told her he would like to take her and Becky to lunch on Sunday; afterward, they could sail on Oakland's Lake Merritt. He wanted Joan to reply right away: he would be leaving soon for New York on a business trip.

He was not feeling well. His kidneys were unable to remove toxins from his blood, and these poisons were killing him. But he did his morning writing, a Hawaiian novel he was calling *Cherry*. He slept most of the afternoon, but when he finally arose, he did not have the energy even to play with his dog Possum. After supper, he had a burst of energy and talked with his stepsister Eliza about his plans for the ranch. He wanted to establish a general store on the property. He planned to have a school, too — perhaps even a post office.

Later, he picked up two boxes of books and papers to take to bed with him. "Look," he said to Charmian, his voice low and lifeless, "see what I've got to read tonight." Exhausted, he lay a while beside her on her couch. They talked for about an hour. Then, standing to leave, he said something surprising: "Thank God, you're not afraid of anything!" It was early in the

evening, perhaps about eight o'clock. He would never
speak to Charmian again. Later, she went outside for a
walk in the starlight and noticed his light was on. Back
inside, she peeked in on him. He appeared to be asleep.

Early the next morning, Eliza entered Charmian's
room and woke her with the startling news that they
had not been able to awaken Jack. When Charmian
rushed to his side, she saw what she called "plain symptoms of poisoning," Jack's kidneys had failed; he was in
a coma. They poured strong coffee down his throat and
sent for doctors. Everyone tried to awaken him. They
called to him and propped him up on his feet.
Charmian, desperate, screamed in his face: "The dam
has burst!" He formed a fist and weakly struck the mat-
tress. Then he slipped back into a coma.

They carried him to Charmian's sleeping porch at
the front of the cottage. From there, if he had opened
his eyes, he could have seen his Beauty Ranch spread
out before him like a dream. But by evening he was gone.

E P I L O G U E

Death, with Jack, had not seemed like
death.
>— Charmian Kittredge London,
> *The Book of Jack London*

Lord, Lord, man! I haven't begun to write
yet.
>— Jack London, letter to Roland Phillips,
> *Cosmopolitan*, March 14, 1913

The doctors who attended Jack London in his final hours all agreed: death was due to uremia, blood poisoning as a result of kidney failure. They all signed a statement to that effect. Physicians today who have looked at Jack's medical records and condition concur. Some believe that he may have suffered a massive stroke, as well. Yet another physician has written that Jack exhibited the symptoms of systemic lupus erythematosus, or lupus — a disease that attacks the connective tissue, then a vital organ like the kidneys. Excessive exposure to sunlight can both trigger it and make it worse.

A story began in the 1930s that Jack had committed suicide. It is a story still published from time to time, even in respectable reference books. It is false. Jack's health was terrible at the end. His body could no longer tolerate the toxins his kidneys could not remove, nor could it take the strain of long sleepless hours and an extremely stressful routine.

Although it is possible that he injected himself that night with morphine (a painkiller) there is no evidence that he took an overdose, intentional or otherwise. Jack routinely medicated himself, as did many people before medical practices became more advanced and before the Food and Drug Administration began to regulate powerful drugs.

On November 23, Jack lay in state in a gray suit at the ranch. The following day his body was cremated in Oakland. Only a month before he died, he had written that "cremation is the only decent, right, sensible way of ridding the world of us when the world has ridden itself of us." There was a funeral service afterward, but Charmian did not attend. She wanted Bessie to go with the children. The girls attended with one of Jack's doctors but Bessie did not go.

On November 26, Jack's friends George Sterling and Ernest Matthews took his ashes to Glen Ellen. They were buried on a little knoll overlooking the Valley of the Moon. Later, a large stone from Wolf House was rolled over the spot. George wrote a poem for his friend. In the final stanza he said:

Farewell! although thou know not, there alone.
Farewell! although thou hear not in our cry
The love we would have given had we known.
Ah! And a soul like thine — how shall it die?

Newspapers all over the world reported Jack's death — often on the front page. The *New York Times* headline read: JACK LONDON DIES SUDDENLY ON RANCH. A long article summarized his life and career. An editorial in the *Cleveland Plain Dealer* spoke for millions of Jack's sorrowful readers: "Many Americans and many men and women of culture throughout the world will feel the death of Jack London as a personal loss."

Jack had written so much that was not yet published that for three years after his death, his stories and articles were still appearing in magazines. In 1917 three of his books were published, another in 1918, yet another in 1919, still another in 1920. A collection of stories for young people, *Dutch Courage*, appeared in 1922. In 1924 Charmian completed and published the novel Jack had been working on the day he died. She changed the name from *Cherry* to *Eyes of Asia.* Jack had left about twenty thousand words of a novel, *The Assassination Bureau, Ltd.*, which another writer, Robert Fish, finished and published in 1963.

Since his death in 1916, Jack's books have been published over and over again in scores of languages in countries all around the globe. Many have been made into radio shows and movies and television shows.

Students all over the world — from elementary school to university graduate school — read, enjoy, and study his works.

Signs of his writing and his life are everywhere. "The call of the wild" is a phrase in our language. On the Oakland waterfront there is a large development of shops and restaurants and bookstores called Jack London Square. His Yukon cabin is there, as is a replica of the *Razzle Dazzle*, the little San Francisco Bay sailboat from his teenage days. Johnny Heinold's First and Last Chance Saloon still serves customers; on the outside wall is a bronze plaque honoring Jack. In Santa Clara, California, there is a plaque on the wall of a monastery. It says that the land behind the wall was once part of Judge Bond's ranch — the ranch Jack used as the opening scene for *The Call of the Wild* and the closing scenes of *White Fang*. In a glass case in the lobby of the National Maritime Museum in San Francisco is a large model of the *Snark*.

In Dawson City, Yukon, is another replica of his Henderson Creek cabin. In the summer, there are readings from his work at the cabin. Tourists sit and listen once again to Jack's words.

In Glen Ellen, California, much of his old Beauty Ranch — about eight hundred acres — is now the Jack London State Historical Park. Visitors can see the ruins of Wolf House. The pig palace, the silos, the dam, the lake, and the bathhouse are still there. Tourists can have a picnic in a grove of eucalyptus trees Jack planted. They can walk through the newly restored cottage, see his study, and stand on Charmian's sleeping porch where he died. They can look out over the fields of grapes still being raised for wine by some of Jack's relatives. They can walk to his grave site. Each year a hundred thousand people visit the ranch.

When Jack died, Charmian built another home on the property. She called it the House of Happy Walls, and she filled it with items they had collected and loved over the years. In 1959, four years after Charmian's death, the House of Happy Walls became a museum for the state park.

Gradually Jack's friends and family passed on. Flora died in 1922, outliving her son by five years. Jennie Prentiss, age ninety, died the same year in a nursing home. In 1925 George Sterling took his own life. Bessie, Jack's first wife, suffered a severe stroke in 1936 and lingered for eleven more years. Jack's stepsister Eliza died in 1939. His friend Ted Applegarth lived until 1964. Jack's daughter Joan passed away in 1971; Becky, in 1992. Until the very end Becky London would eagerly talk with anyone about her memories of the man she called "Daddy" all her life.

Jack London died at forty. But he had achieved much in so short a time. He had written fifty books and hundreds of stories and articles. He had sailed halfway around the world and had designed and operated a model ranch. He had fought hard for the poor and the underprivileged. He had supported those whom he loved and had been a devoted friend.

"The thing I like most of all," Jack wrote, "is

personal achievement — not achievement for the world's applause, but achievement for my own delight." On the night he died, in his last lucid moments, if he did indeed remember his many achievements, he surely must have felt supreme delight. He would have been pleased to know that the world's applause for all he had done — for all he had *been* — would continue for a long, long time.

ACKNOWLEDGMENTS AND PHOTO CREDITS

In this biography I have attempted to stick to verified facts about Jack London's life. This is not always easy. So many legends about him have grown during the years since his death that it is difficult, at times, to separate what really happened from what might have happened. While he was alive, Jack himself was occasionally guilty of adding to the legend by exaggerating his accomplishments.

I have been aided in this sifting process by a number of important books — especially Jack London's own letters (he wrote thousands of them) and his own autobiographical writing. Jack's second wife, Charmian, wrote a biography of her husband, as did his daughter Joan. Both have been very helpful. Some people who knew him also wrote accounts of their experiences. Martin Johnson traveled with the Londons on the *Snark*, and Georgia Loring Bamford knew Jack in high school.

Perhaps most useful of all have been two works by the late Russ Kingman, *A Pictorial Life of Jack London* and *Jack London: A Definitive Chronology*. Russ devoted most of his adult life to establishing the facts of Jack London's life, and every London biographer owes him an enormous debt. His wife, Winnie, has continued to provide materials and information to London fans and scholars from the enormous files the Kingmans have assembled over the years. She has been essential in the creation of this book.

In many cases I have tried to let Jack and those who knew him speak for themselves. I have not cluttered the story with footnotes, but there is a complete list of references at the end of the book.

I would like to thank some of the many people who contributed to this work directly and indirectly. The Huntington Library in San Marino, California, maintains the most extensive collection of Jack London material in the world. I have spent many, many hours in the Huntington and have always been grateful for the quick, professional response from all the librarians, especially Sarah Hodson.

I. Milo Shepard, Jack London's great-nephew and trustee of the estate of Irving Shepard, has, as usual, been generous and considerate as I proceeded on this volume. With his help I was able to examine original manuscripts and photographs and diaries in the Huntington collections. In 1990 I was honored to have a fascinating afternoon's conversation with Becky London, Jack's daughter.

Earle Labor is without question the world's greatest authority on Jack London, and I have benefitted over and over from his advice and help. I want to thank, as well, Clarice Stasz, Susan Nuernberg, Dorothy Hershberger, David Mike Hamilton, and members of the Jack London Network on the Internet — all have answered questions, small and large, quickly and authoritatively.

The San Francisco Public Library sent copies of materials from its microfilm archives, and the Hudson Library and Historical Society (Hudson, Ohio) was extremely accommodating with my many inter-library loan requests. William Sturm in the Oakland History Room of the Oakland Main Library is a superior librarian — expert and wise — and I wish to thank, as well, the staff at the Bancroft Library at the University of California at Berkeley where I spent a very productive day.

My students and colleagues in the Aurora (Ohio) City Schools — and at Harmon School, in particular — have been, as always, encouraging in all that I do. I would like to thank, especially, Jerry Brodsky, Burke Stephens, James Costanza, and the members of the Board of Education for their unwavering support.

Finally, friends and family continue to provide the foundation of affection upon which I build. Claude and Dorothy Steele kept the door open for me at Stanford. And thank you — again and again and again — to Mom and Dad, Steve, Richard, Dave, Janice, Ricky, and Bella. And Joyce . . . nothing at all happens in my life without you.

PHOTO CREDITS

BIBLIOGRAPHY

I. By Jack London — Original Editions

The Son of the Wolf. Boston: Houghton, Mifflin, 1900.

The God of His Fathers. New York: McClure, Phillips, 1901.

Children of the Frost. New York: Macmillan, 1902.

The Cruise of the "Dazzler." New York: Century, 1902.

A Daughter of the Snows. Philadelphia: J. B. Lippincott, 1902.

The Kempton-Wace Letters [with Anna Strunsky]. New York: Macmillan, 1903.

The Call of the Wild. New York: Macmillan, 1903.

The People of the Abyss. New York: Macmillan, 1903.

The Faith of Men. New York: Macmillan, 1904.

The Sea-Wolf. New York: Macmillan, 1904.

War of the Classes. New York: Macmillan, 1905.

The Game. New York: Macmillan, 1905.

Tales of the Fish Patrol. New York: Macmillan, 1905.

Moon-Face and Other Stories. New York: Macmillan, 1906.

White Fang. New York: Macmillan, 1906.

Scorn of Women. New York: Macmillan, 1906.

Before Adam. New York: Macmillan, 1907.

Love of Life and Other Stories. New York: Macmillan 1907.

The Road. New York: Macmillan, 1907.

The Iron Heel. New York: Macmillan, 1907.

Martin Eden. New York: Macmillan, 1909.

Lost Face. New York: Macmillan, 1910.

Revolution and Other Essays. New York: Macmillan, 1910.

Burning Daylight. New York: Macmillan, 1910.

Theft: A Play in Four Acts. New York: Macmillan, 1910.

When God Laughs and Other Stories. New York: Macmillan, 1911.

Adventure. New York: Macmillan, 1911.

The Cruise of the "Snark." New York: Macmillan, 1911.

South Sea Tales. New York: Macmillan, 1911.

The House of Pride and Other Tales of Hawaii. New York: Macmillan, 1912.

The Son of the Sun. Garden City, N. Y.: Doubleday, Page, 1912.

Smoke Bellew. New York: Century, 1912.

The Night-Born. New York: Century, 1913.

The Abysmal Brute. New York: Century, 1913.

John Barleycorn. New York: Century, 1913.

The Valley of the Moon. New York: Macmillan, 1913.

The Strength of the Strong. New York: Macmillan, 1914.

The Mutiny of the "Elsinore." New York: Macmillan, 1914.

The Scarlet Plague. New York: Macmillan, 1915.

The Star Rover. New York: Macmillan, 1915.

The Acorn-Planter: A California Forest Play. New York: Macmillan, 1916.

The Little Lady of the Big House. New York: Macmillan, 1916.

The Turtles of Tasman. New York: Macmillan, 1916.

The Human Drift. New York: Macmillan, 1917.

Jerry of the Islands. New York: Macmillan, 1917.

Michael, Brother of Jerry. New York: Macmillan, 1917.

The Red One. New York: Macmillan, 1918.

On the Makaloa Mat. New York: Macmillan, 1919.

Hearts of Three. New York: Macmillan, 1920.

Dutch Courage and Other Stories. New York: Macmillan, 1922.

The Assassination Bureau, Ltd. Completed by Robert L. Fish. New York: McGraw-Hill, 1963.

II. By Jack London — Collections

The Complete Short Stories of Jack London. Edited by Earle
   Labor, Robert C. Leitz III, and I. Milo Shepard. 3 vols.
   Stanford, Calif.: Stanford University Press, 1993.

Jack London in the "Aegis." Edited by James Sisson III.
   Oakland, Calif.: Star Rover House, 1980.

*Jack London on the Road: The Tramp Diary and Other Hobo
   Writings.* Edited by Richard W. Etulain. Logan: Utah State
   University Press, 1979.

Jack London Reports. Edited by King Hendricks and Irving
   Shepard. New York: Doubleday, 1970.

The Letters of Jack London. Edited by Earle Labor, Robert C.
   Leitz III, and I. Milo Shepard. 3 vols. Stanford, Calif.:
   Stanford University Press, 1988.

The Portable Jack London. Edited by Earle Labor. New York:
   Penguin, 1994.

Short Stories: Authorized Edition with Definitive Texts. Edited by
   Earle Labor, Robert C. Leitz III and I. Milo Shepard. New
   York: Macmillan, 1990.

Tales of Adventure. Edited by Irving Shepard. Garden City,
   N. Y.: Hanover House, 1956.

III. About Jack London

Atherton, Frank. *Jack London in Boyhood Adventures.*
   Unpublished manuscript.

Bamford, Georgia Loring. *The Mystery of Jack London.*
   Oakland, Calif.: Privately printed, 1931.

Day, A. Grove. *Jack London in the South Seas.* New York: Four
   Winds Press, 1971.

Eames, Ninetta. "Jack London." *Overland Monthly* 35 (May 1900): 417-25.

Hamilton, David Mike. *"The Tools of My Trade": Annotated Books in Jack London's Library.* Seattle: University of Washington Press, 1986.

Haughey, Homer L., and Connie Kale Johnson. *Jack London Ranch Album.* Stockton, Calif.: Heritage, 1985.

———. *Jack London Homes Album.* Stockton, Calif.: Heritage, 1987.

Hershberger, Dorothy J. "Flora Wellman: The Early Years." Paper presented at the annual meeting of the Popular Culture Association, 1995.

Johnson, Martin. *Through the South Seas with Jack London.* New York: Dodd, Mead, 1913. Reprint. Cedar Springs, Mich.: Wolf House Books, 1972.

Johnston, Carolyn. *Jack London — An American Radical?* Westport, Conn.: Greenwood, 1984.

Kingman, Russ. *Jack London: A Definitive Chronology.* Middletown, Calif.: David Rejl, 1992.

———. *A Pictorial Life of Jack London.* New York: Crown, 1979.

Labor, Earle, and Jeanne Campbell Reesman. *Jack London.* Revised edition. New York: Twayne, 1994.

Lasartemay, Eugene P., and Mary Rudge. *For Love of Jack London: His Life with Jennie Prentiss — A True Love Story.* New York: Vantage Press, 1991.

London, Charmian Kittredge. *The Book of Jack London.* 2 vols. New York: Century, 1921.

————. *The Log of the* "Snark." New York: Macmillan, 1915.

————. *Our Hawaii.* New York: Macmillan, 1917. Revised edition, 1922.

London, Joan. *Jack London and His Daughters.* Berkeley, Calif.: Heyday Books, 1990.

————. *Jack London and His Times.* New York: Doubleday, 1939. Reprint, with a new introduction by the author. Seattle: University of Washington Press, 1968.

Mood, Fulmer. "An Astrologer from Down East." *New England Quarterly* 5 (1932): 769-799.

Noel, Joseph. *Footloose in Arcadia: A Personal Record of Jack London, George Sterling, Ambrose Bierce.* New York: Carrick & Evans, 1940.

North, Dick. *Jack London's Cabin.* Whitehorse, Yukon: Willow Printers, 1986.

Sinclair, Andrew. *Jack: A Biography of Jack London.* New York: Harper & Row, 1977.

Stasz, Clarice. *American Dreamers: Charmian and Jack London.* New York: St. Martin's Press, 1988.

Stone, Irving. *Sailor on Horseback: The Biography of Jack London.* Cambridge, Mass.: Houghton Mifflin, 1938.

Thompson, Fred. "Diary of Yukon Experiences with Jack London, Mr. Shepard, Merritt Sloper, Jim Goodman, July–October 1897." Henry E. Huntington Library, San Marino, Calif.

Walker, Franklin. *Jack London and the Klondike: The Genesis of an American Writer.* San Marino, Calif.: Huntington Library, 1966.

Wearin, Otha Donner. *Heinold's First and Last Chance: Jack London's Rendezvous*. Second edition. Privately printed, 1987.

Williams, Tony. *Jack London — The Movies*. Middletown, Calif.: David Rejl, 1992.

Zamen, Mark E. *Standing Room Only: Jack London's Controversial Career as a Public Speaker*. New York: Peter Lang, 1990.

IV. General Reference

Berton, Pierre. *Klondike: The Last Great Gold Rush, 1896–1899*. Revised edition. Toronto: McClelland and Stewart Limited, 1985.

Schlereth, Thomas J. *Victorian America: Transformations in Everyday Life, 1876–1915*. New York: HarperCollins, 1991.

Schwantes, Carlos A. *Coxey's Army: An American Odyssey*. Lincoln: University of Nebraska Press, 1985.

Slocum, Joshua. *Sailing Alone Around the World*. New York: Century, 1900.

INDEX

Page references in italics indicate photographs. References to individual works written by Jack London can be found under London, Jack: Works.